LINCOLN CHRISTIAN COLLEGE

P9-CQM-113

WHEN Anger Hurts YOUR RELATIONSHIP

10 SIMPLE SOLUTIONS FOR COUPLES WHO FIGHT

KIM PALEG, PH.D
MATTHEW MCKAY, PH.D.

NEW HARBINGER PUBLICATIONS, INC.

Publisher's Note

This publication is designed to provide accurate and authoritative information in regard to the subject matter covered. It is sold with the understanding that the publisher is not engaged in rendering psychological, financial, legal, or other professional services. If expert assistance or counseling is needed, the services of a competent professional should be sought.

Distributed in the U.S.A. by Publishers Group West; in Canada by Raincoast Books; in Great Britain by Airlift Book Company, Ltd.; in South Africa by Real Books, Ltd.; in Australia by Boobook; and in New Zealand by Tandem Press.

Copyright © 2001 by Matthew McKay and Kim Paleg
New Harbinger Publications, Inc.
5674 Shattuck Avenue
Oakland, CA 94609

Cover design by SHELBY DESIGNS & ILLUSTRATES
Edited by Heather Garnos
Text design by Michele Waters

Library of Congress Catalog Card Number: 01-132292
ISBN 1-57224-260-4 Paperback

All Rights Reserved

Printed in the United States of America

New Harbinger Publications' Web site address: www.newharbinger.com

03   02   01

10   9   8   7   6   5   4   3   2   1

First printing

For my son, Jordan, with love.
—MM

For Tom Boyd, with love.
—KP

103445

Contents

Introduction

The Anger Trap

Anger is fueled by pain: hurt, shame, fear, frustration, guilt, threats to self-esteem, back/head/neck ache. You name it, virtually any kind of emotional or physical distress can be an anger trigger. Anger can help to control pain in two ways. One, it discharges, in a burst of angry energy, a lot of the physiological arousal that pain generates. Two, because anger is such a big and dramatic emotion, it can mask other very painful feelings. Think back to the last time your partner criticized you. Wasn't there a moment—before you got angry—where you just felt hurt or guilty or wrong? That's painful as hell. So along came the anger to discharge or block the pain.

Angry people have three things in common: (1) they're in a lot of pain, (2) they feel helpless to do anything about the causes of the pain, and (3) they have learned, usually in their family of origin, to get angry as a way to temporarily mask the pain. But here's how you get trapped. Anger only works for a little while. The guilt or shame or hurt will come back. Something your partner says retriggers it, or your own thoughts may set off feelings of shame and unworthiness. So you have to get angry again to stop it. Your partner, meanwhile, doesn't take to the role of punching bag. He or she is getting hurt—and angry. And takes revenge by withdrawing, withholding, criticizing, or blaming. All of which triggers more pain in you that you have to block with another angry outburst.

The anger cycle keeps spinning and digging your relationship deeper in a hole. Pain → anger, pain → anger, pain → anger. It just goes on. Getting hurt and blowing up; your partner doing the same. You're both trapped because anger, no matter how right and legitimate it feels, is a short-term solution. In the long run it begets more suffering.

Anger as a Defense

When a partner is frustrating you, shaming you, guilting you, or blaming you, the pain is often so great that you want to punish them. You want revenge. If you could only pay them back, if there were only some justice, you sense that it would ease the pain. So you slap them with your words. You try to make them feel the same guilt and shame and wrongness you do. You withhold so they'll feel the emotional hunger that lives inside of you. You cut them down to be as small as you sometimes feel.

It's so instinctive: punish the one who hurts you. And right along with that impulse is the deep-seated belief that you'll feel better, that vengeance will heal you. But it's a myth. The relief, if any, is temporary and soon replaced by another round of hurts. You know that because you've tried punishment; there have been moments where all you wanted was to emotionally destroy your partner. Every word from your mouth was a bullet aimed for the heart. But none of it made you feel better. Not for long. You are reading this book because you're still in pain, still looking for a way out.

The anger, the will to punish, props you up and defends you for a moment. Then you crash again. The relief is an illusion. The only real escape is to stop using anger—and punishment—as a means of protection. How do you do this? How do you reverse a pattern learned when you were young? The answer is one day at a time. This book is packed with proven techniques that will work for you.

How to Use This Book

Each of the ten chapters in this book can be used independently to reduce the conflict in your relationship. Better yet, they can be combined to achieve total victory over destructive anger.

Combined, these chapters offer skills that can be applied in three stages: (1) *prevention* of future anger episodes, (2) *management* when an episode threatens to escalate, and (3) *repair* after you've slipped into old patterns.

The prevention chapters include (1) Make a Contract (where you swear off anger one day at a time), (2) Relax Away Your Anger (where you learn to release tension using Cue-Controlled Relaxation while stopping upsetting thoughts with the Eye Movement Technique), (3) Understand Your Partner's Feelings (where you practice Empathy Training using the Couple's Research Form and the technique of Role Reversal), (4) Be Angry Respectfully (where you learn to use assertive I Statements to ask for what you want), and (5) Watch Out for the Four Don'ts (where you learn to avoid "The Four Horsemen of the Apocalypse"—criticism, contempt, defensiveness, and stonewalling).

The management chapters include (6) Learn to De-Escalate (where you use the Repair Checklist to calm down and break the angry impasse), (7) Try Time Out and Negotiation (where you use the structured Time Out exercise to prevent a blowup and prepare for later Negotiation steps), and (9) Create an Anger Coping Plan (that synthesizes all your new skills into a step-by-step plan to change chronic anger patterns).

The repair chapters help you rebuild trust and closeness in your relationship, and include (8) Change the Way You Speak (where you learn a powerful new technique called Language Reform), and (10) Give Your Partner Pleasure (where you can reverse years of distancing with the Pleasure Exchange).

We suggest you start with Make a Contract to get twenty-four hours of relief from anger. Then master Time Out (chapter 7) to make sure new conflicts don't escalate into relationship-scarring events. Once you're able to stop anger in its tracks, you can work on Relaxation (chapter 2) and Empathy Building (chapter 3). From there on, we suggest you choose a chapter from the Management section, then one from the Repair group, and finally back again to Prevention. Repeat this sequence till you've finished the book.

You will find that this book takes work—and commitment. But the rewards are great. If you really do the exercises and practice the new skills, your relationship will change deeply and fundamentally. Not only will you have less pain, but you will feel, without the lacerations of constant anger, closer than any time since your first, sweet days together.

CHAPTER 1

Make a Contract

What Is an Anger Contract?

Breaking out of the anger trap starts with a simple commitment: today you will act in a calm, nonaggressive way. Forget the blowup last week where you threw the plate, forget the harsh exchange of expletives last night, forget even what happened twenty minutes ago. None of that matters. It's the past. This moment, the eternal present, is all that counts. Because this is where all decisions are made; this is where change is created.

How can a commitment to act calmly be successful? After all, you've probably tried to change how you express anger many times. And you picked up this book because it's still a problem, still damaging your relationship. There are three ways you can be successful now, even if you've never had much luck controlling angry behavior before.

1. You don't have to *be* calm—just *act* calm. It's a lot easier to control behavior than feelings. Commit yourself to functioning *as if* you were calm and relaxed, no matter how provoked you feel. In this case, how you look and how you sound are all that matter.

2. Stay aware of what anger is costing you. What's the number one price you pay for angry behavior with your partner? Coldness and withdrawal, loss of sexual intimacy, attacks on your self-esteem, damage to your kids, loss of trust, loss of the spirit of help and cooperation? Right now, visualize a scene from the recent past that epitomizes the cost of your anger. This should be a touchstone, an image you can use to motivate and remind yourself to behave calmly. Visualize this scene every morning as you start your day—perhaps as you shave or put on your makeup. Then recommit yourself to looking and sounding calm throughout the day.

3. Promise to be calm for twenty-four hours at a time. The chapter section titled "How to Use It" will describe, step-by-step, how to make effective anger contracts with your partner.

Where Does It Come From, and Is It Effective?

The one-day-at-a-time approach to impulse management was pioneered by the Twelve-Step movement. Success with making twenty-four hour goals was first reported in Alcoholics Anonymous (AA) literature dating back to the 1930s. Nearly seventy years of use, in Twelve-Step groups all over the world, has proven that twenty-four-hour commitments are easier to manage and maintain than open-ended behavior management goals.

The specific, twenty-four-hour contract used here was developed by anger expert, Ron Potter-Efron, and first described in his book *Angry All the Time*. It has helped tens of thousands of angry people worldwide.

Twenty-four-hour anger commitments are effective because the key to changing any pattern is to work at it intensively for a brief period of time. You've got to be thinking about it, staying vigilant and trying hard. But you can't keep that effort up for long. A month wouldn't work. Not even a week. You'd soon start forgetting how vital the commitment is. You'd get distracted by other things. You'd stop being so hyperaware of your behavior and any early warning signs that you're starting to lose it. The answer: make the commitment and go all out to keep it for one day. And if you choose, do exactly the same thing on day two, day three, and so on.

How to Use It

Here's how you structure a brief anger contract:

1. Tell your partner that you're committed to acting calm for twenty-four hours. It's also helpful to share this with close friends and trusted members of your family. The more people who know about your commitment, the stronger it will feel. Explain that between _____ and _____, you won't hit, shout at, swear at, blame, attack, or denigrate your partner—no matter what your partner does, and no matter how provoked you feel. Tell your partner, friends, and family that you plan to pay attention and be on guard against angry behavior throughout the entire period.

2. Ask for your partner's help. Give him or her a nonverbal signal that can be used to let you know when you're starting to go over the line. If you see the signal, let it act as a "red flag" to stop aggression in its tracks. Stop talking for a moment until you can recover the *appearance* of being calm. Remember, you don't have to feel calm—just look it.

3. Sign a written contract with your partner. An example appears below of a twenty-four-hour commitment, and there are additional copies at the end of the chapter. You can make photocopies or copy the contact in your notebook or on a separate sheet of paper. Notice that your partner signs as a witness.

Twenty-Four-Hour Commitment

I _____ , between _____

o'clock on _____ and _____
       (date)

o'clock on _____ , promise to behave
       (date)

in a calm, nonaggressive manner. I will act calmly no matter what stress or provocation may occur.

_____
Your signature

_____
Witness—your partner's signature

---

4. See the benefit. Go back for a moment to the scene you visualized that symbolizes what anger costs you in your relationship. Now turn it around. Imagine a positive counterpart to that scene that could be achieved by controlling anger. Visualize a moment of warmth, or sexual intimacy, or help and support. Spend some time imagining it—how you would touch, how you would talk to each other. And notice how it might feel to recover an experience that likely was part of your early relationship.

5. Anticipate provocations. Scan ahead for situations you might encounter during the next twenty-four hours. Are there shared tasks you might struggle with? Is there a stressor that might trigger anger for either you or your partner? Is there an unresolved issue that keeps cropping up? Are there predictable irritants (e.g., a partner being late, food preparation styles, chore responsibilities, parenting tasks) that might arise in the coming day? Whatever comes up, you'll need a coping strategy. Copy the following worksheet into your notebook, and list the

likely provocations in the left-hand column. (You'll fill in the right-hand column after you read the next section.)

Anger Provocation Worksheet

Expected Provocation   **Coping Response**

1. _____   _____

2. _____   _____

3. _____   _____

4. _____   _____

5. _____   _____

Staying Calm When You Get Angry

The number one thing to do when you start getting angry is to shut up. Don't say anything that's driven by anger. Tell your partner, "Just a moment, I need to think this through." Then either go into another room or physically walk away for a minute.

During the break, remind yourself that this is just an emotion. It doesn't have to control you. It's like a wave on the ocean—no matter how high and fast, it always passes. There's a trough of calm on the other side. How long would the wave of anger last if you didn't somehow feed it? Five minutes? Thirty? An hour? You can get through that.

Now step back from the feeling and label it. There's more going on than simple anger. Remember how anger is often used to mask other painful emotions? What feelings do you have besides anger—hurt, frustration, shame, despair that things will never change? Say to yourself, "I'm angry, but underneath it I feel _____ ." Don't start talking again until you are aware of at least one other feeling that your anger's trying to hide. And when you do start talking, describe the hidden feeling to your partner—not the anger.

Stop making a case for how wrong and bad your partner is. Or how much they've hurt you. This just feeds the anger and reduces your ability to stay calm. Focus instead on coping. Are there calming thoughts that could reduce the anger wave's size? Here are some coping thoughts that have helped others stay calm when provoked (McKay and Rogers 2000):

- Just as long as I keep my cool, I'm in control.

- Take a deep breath and relax.

- Easy does it—there's nothing to be gained in getting mad.

- Getting upset won't help.

- I'm not going to let him/her get to me.

- I can't change him/her with anger; I'll just upset myself.

- I can find a way to say what I want without anger.

- Stay calm—no sarcasm, no attacks.

- I can stay calm and relaxed.

- Relax and let go. No need to get my knickers in a twist.

- No one is right, no one is wrong. We just have different needs.

- His/her needs are as important as mine. We can figure this out together.

- Stay cool, make no judgments.

- No matter what is said, I know I'm a good person.

- I'll stay rational—anger won't solve anything.

- Punishment won't work; nothing changes.

- I can shrug off the criticism; I won't be pushed into losing my cool.

- Bottom line, I'm in control. I'm out of here rather than say or do something dumb.

- Some situations don't have good solutions. Looks like this is one of them. No use getting all bent out of shape about it.

- It's just a hassle. Nothing more, nothing less. I can cope with hassles.

- It's just not worth it to get all angry.

- I can manage this; I'm in control.

- If they want me to get angry, I'm going to disappoint them.

- I can't expect people to act the way I want them to.

- I don't have to take this so seriously.

- Let it go, let it go.

- We're both trying to cope with something difficult. I can stay cool and let things work themselves out.

Select a couple of the above coping thoughts that seem like they might work for you. Or make a few of your own. Write one in the Coping Response column of the Anger Provocation Worksheet for each anticipated anger trigger.

Also in the Coping Response column, write down the feeling(s) that usually underlie your anger in that situation. Commit yourself to staying aware of them, and decide not to cover them with rage. Now write in anything else that you might say or do in the situation to de-escalate things and help you stay calm. Could you acknowledge your partner's pain and struggle? Could you suggest talking later when you've both cooled down? Is there a possible solution to the problem you can think of now?

Acting Calm

One of the best ways to change how you feel is to act the opposite. During your twenty-four-hour commitment to calm behavior, we urge you to follow these five guidelines (McKay and Rogers 2000):

1. Smile instead of frown. The process of shifting your face into a smile has the effect of dissipating negative feelings. It also signals to your partner that you're not upset, so there is no need for them to put on any psychological armor.

2. Speak softly rather than loudly. This is really crucial. Go out of your way to make your voice gentler than usual. The more soothing you sound, the less you risk escalation.

3. Relax instead of tighten. Slump in your chair, lean against a wall, uncross your arms, let your shoulders sag a little. Give the appearance of calm and control, even if you feel like you need riot police for what's going on inside.

4. Disengage rather than attack. Look or walk away if things are heating up. Ask for time to collect yourself. Save critical comments for another time. Stop trying to fix things or be understood.

5. Empathize rather than judge. Say something mildly supportive, even if it feels phony. Tell your partner that you can appreciate his or her concerns, and that you'd like to work out something that feels good to both of you.

Why Is This a One-Sided Commitment?

It might seem unfair, on the face of it, that the promise to remain calm is made unilaterally by one partner, instead of both to each other. And it might seem that the blame for all the anger in the relationship is now being shouldered by the partner who signs the contract. But there are reasons the twenty-four-hour commitment is structured the way it is. First of all, you have to take 100 percent responsibility for controlling your own anger. No matter what your partner does or says, you need to remain calm. If the contract were a mutual agreement, and your partner in some way provoked you, that might seem grounds for vacating the contract and giving up on your own commitment to be calm. With a unilateral contract, your commitment should remain unaffected by *any* of your partner's behavior.

The second reason for a unilateral contract is that both partners may not be ready to acknowledge that they have an anger problem. If that's the case, the requirement of a mutual contract would effectively block any progress with anger control. Signing the contract doesn't mean you take total responsibility for all the anger in the relationship—just for your anger during the next twenty-four hours.

The third reason is that you can, if you wish to, sign two contracts—both of you promising to stay calm for a day. But don't get hung up on waiting for or expecting that. The important thing is that *one* of you starts to reverse the old patterns of anger by making this brief commitment.

What Happens After Twenty-Four Hours?

Basically there are two choices: (1) make an additional twenty-four-hour commitment, signed and sealed by both of you, or (2) immediately implement one of the other nine strategies in this book. Doing neither isn't a choice. Your relationship has already been scarred by anger, and you've got to stop more damage from being done. So keep making one-day contracts until you've learned enough to seriously try other anger control methods.

Example: Harlen and Corey

Harlen and Corey were at a point where the fighting was a daily occurrence—and often quite vicious. The main issue had to do with Corey's emotional coolness. She was a family law attorney who worked long hours when she was litigating. She found Harlen's emotional and sexual needs to be overwhelming when she got home. Their relationship had fallen into the classic pursuer-distancer pattern where Harlen would snipe and guilt-trip Corey because she often wanted to read and relax, rather than engage with him.

Dinner was a real ulcer fest because Harlen could finally get Corey's attention and lambaste her for being late and unavailable, and generally giving him less love than he wanted. Corey would respond finally by pointing out that Harlen had no real friends and ought to stop complaining and go get a life. These wars would continue until Corey withdrew to bed and Harlen went off to sulk in front of the television.

After reading about anger contracts, Harlen made a decision that the fighting had to stop. He told Corey about his desire to get through at least one day without anger, and then see where to go from there. He gave her a signal she could use (a referee's time-out sign) and promised to stop any angry behavior if she used it.

Harlen then signed a Twenty-Four-Hour Commitment and Corey countersigned as his witness. They both agreed that making a formal, signed contract increased the seriousness of the promise. Harlen also shared with his dad what was going on, and promised to give him an update the next day on how it turned out.

Harlen worked to increase his resolve by visualizing the last day of their trip to Carmel—all the bitterness and estrangement after spending the whole week of their vacation fighting. The drive home was like taking a swim in the Barents Sea. Lots of icebergs. He remembered it well, and visualized it on the morning of his daylong commitment.

On the Anger Provocation Worksheet, Harlen listed three possibilities: (1) if Corey was significantly late getting home, (2) if she spent more than an hour wrapped up in her novel and left him alone in the kitchen cooking dinner, and (3) if she went to bed without any conversation or at least an affectionate "good night." His planned coping responses included: (1) reminding himself he could get through the wave of pain, (2) labeling the underlying feelings of hurt and disappointment, (3) telling Corey about the hurt in a calm way, (4) using the coping thought, "punishing her won't work; nothing changes," and (5) acknowledging how emotionally spent Corey must be after work.

One additional thing Harlen decided to do was keep his voice soft. He knew it got a loud edge when he was starting up the anger ladder, so he planned to stay hyperaware of how loudly he was talking.

The twenty-four-hour period started at six P.M. Harlen was nervous that his anger would be triggered if Corey were late getting home. She was, in fact, nearly an hour late, and he had to really work for a few minutes at looking and sounding calm. He reminded himself that punishing her wouldn't work, and forced himself to say that she must feel really tired.

Problems continued when Corey collapsed onto the couch and started reading her Agatha Christie novel. Harlen pulled the dinner together, but was starting to get hot. With a real effort, he reminded himself of the feelings underneath his anger: hurt and disappointment. And as Corey came in for dinner, he mentioned mildly that he was a little disappointed that she hadn't visited with him while he was cooking.

Corey had a little "here we go again" look on her face when she heard that, but actually apologized. Harlen's effort to be calm paid off during dinner because they both seemed on good behavior, chatting pleasantly about various idiots running for office.

Bedtime was another little crisis because Corey slipped off without saying good night. Harlen felt a surge of abandonment, then anger. He labeled the feeling and reminded himself that he could get through the wave. When he finally crawled into bed, he was quiet so as not to wake her. Then, to his surprise, Corey turned to him and kissed him. "Tonight was such a relief," she said.

What If It Fails?

The Anger Contract is a terrific way to tamp down your angry reactions. If you honor the agreement you make with yourself, you will see results—quickly.

Twenty-Four-Hour Commitment

I _____ , between _____

o'clock on _____ and _____
              (date)
o'clock on _____ , promise to behave
              (date)

in a calm, nonaggressive manner. I will act calmly no matter what stress or provocation may occur.

_____
Your signature

_____
Witness—your partner's signature

Twenty-Four-Hour Commitment

I _____ , between _____

o'clock on _____ and _____
              (date)
o'clock on _____ , promise to behave
              (date)

in a calm, nonaggressive manner. I will act calmly no matter what stress or provocation may occur.

_____
Your signature

_____
Witness—your partner's signature

CHAPTER 2

Relax Away Your Anger

What Is Relaxation?

Relaxation is an antidote to anger. All kinds of research shows that it works. But there are two things you need to learn to effectively relax: you have to let go of physical tension in your muscles, and you need to shut off tension-generating thoughts. In this chapter you'll first learn to relax your muscles with a technique called *Stop and Breathe,* and later with a powerful tool called *Cue-Controlled Breathing.* After getting good at physically releasing tension, you can learn to stop negative, anger-generating thoughts with a new strategy called *Eye Movement Technique.* You can learn all of these pretty quickly, so let's get started.

Where Does It Come From, and Is It Effective?

The Stop and Breathe technique was developed by Matthew McKay. It grows out of an earlier Thought Stopping treatment created by Joseph Wolpe in the 1950s and yoga breathing traditions. Stop and Breathe uses *diaphragmatic breathing* which has been proven effective as a relaxation tool in hundreds of clinical studies. Behavioral therapists have been using deep, diaphragmatic breathing to help people relax for nearly fifty years. Cue-Controlled Breathing was developed by a researcher named Ost and has been demonstrated effective in clinical studies. Eye Movement Technique grew out of EMDR (Eye Movement Desensitization and Reprocessing). Research shows that it's effective at stopping negative thoughts for about seven out of ten people (Smyth 1999).

When to Use It

Use your relaxation techniques *before* your anger gets out of control. We'll discuss later in the chapter how to notice "red flag" behaviors that should trigger your relaxation efforts.

Stopping negative thoughts is also crucial, and we'll help you identify key negative thoughts about your partner that you can interrupt using Eye Movement Technique.

How to Use the Relaxation Techniques

Anybody who struggles with anger knows that it makes you incredibly tense. Noradrenaline surges through your bloodstream and drives you to take action—shout, shove, hit—anything to get rid of what threatens or offends you.

Emergency anger control depends, in part, on learning to reverse this process. With a little practice, you can actually relax your body when provoked. And your relaxed muscles can send an "all clear" message to your brain that the threat is past. It will only take you a few minutes to master the first basic technique: Stop and Breathe.

Stop and Breathe

There are three steps to Stop and Breathe. The first is to identify the problem behavior that will be your signal to use the technique. Think about it for a minute. When you get angry at your partner, what are the telltale things you do that lead up to an explosion? Do you raise your voice? Make sarcastic, belittling comments? Do you use foul language? Criticize? How about slamming things around? In the space below or in your notebook, write between two and four behaviors to be used as red flags that an anger outburst is imminent.

Stop and Breathe Worksheet

1. _____

2. _____

3. _____

4. _____

Right now, commit yourself to staying vigilant for the red flag behaviors and using Stop and Breathe when you notice them.

The second step in the Stop and Breathe technique is to *hold everything*. Don't say another word. And stop your anger-fueling thoughts about how mean or wrong or unjust your partner is. Use this coping thought: "I have a choice. I'm not going to get angry." Now disengage. Tell your partner that you need a moment to pull yourself together. Physically, move away. Or at least look away.

The last step in Stop and Breathe is to take four diaphragmatic breaths, counting each out-breath. In other words, you take a breath and exhale, counting one; take another breath and exhale, counting two, and so on up to the count of four, where you have the option to start over.

You can learn diaphragmatic breathing by putting one hand on your chest and the other over your abdomen, just above the belt line. As you take a deep breath, push the air all the way down into your belly. The hand over your abdomen should rise, while the hand on your chest should barely move. Each time you breathe, put all your attention on your belly. Try to send the breath all the way to the bottom. As you complete an in-breath, allow it to slightly stretch and relax your diaphragm. Keep breathing now, watching how your belly rises and falls, and noticing the sense of calmness that steals over you.

Deep, diaphragmatic breathing is faster and safer than taking a Valium. As you stretch your diaphragm and stomach, you send a message to the emotional centers of your brain that all is well. Keep practicing now for a little while until a diaphragmatic breath feels easy and natural.

If you're having any difficulty pushing the air down into your belly, try pressing on your abdomen with both hands, or place a telephone book over your stomach. Then concentrate on using the breath to push up your hands or the phone book.

Diaphragmatic Breathing during Stress

You now know how to take a diaphragmatic breath. But that isn't enough. For Stop and Breathe to help you, you need to master diaphragmatic breathing when you're actually upset about something. In the next exercise, you'll visualize a typical anger-provoking scene with your partner—something on a moderate level. You'll break the scene down into a four-step sequence. For the first step, write down the early stages of the problem that started to get you hot. The second step consists of noting any negative thoughts you had about your partner and how you expressed them. The third step and the fourth are to describe how the fight escalated, culminating in what you said and did when you were angriest.

Breathing during Stress Worksheet

Break the scene down into four segments. In your notebook or in the space below, fill in enough detail to allow you to fully imagine the upsetting event.

1. _____

_____

_____ (deep breath)

2. _____

_____

_____ (deep breath)

3. _____

_____

_____ (deep breath)

4. _____

_____

_____ (deep breath)

Not every anger scene fits exactly into the structure described above. Don't worry about it. Just make sure that you break the scene down into four steps in a sequence. Always include your negative thoughts as well as behavior.

Notice there's a cue for you to take a deep breath after each segment of the scene. You're going to use that in a minute to help you practice diaphragmatic breathing. But right now, run through all four steps in the scene without diaphragmatic breaths. Just focus on each upsetting detail, each negative thought, each offending comment, until you feel good and angry. Notice the tension in your body.

Now go back and visualize each step of the scene, but include the diaphragmatic breath. Repeat this two or three more times. Notice the contrast in tension level between the first time you visualized the scene, without breathing, and later run-throughs that include diaphragmatic breaths. Chances are your body feels very different when you use the deep breaths.

What follows is a sample Breathing During Stress exercise completed by a man who gets enraged when his wife interrupts their dinner with lengthy phone calls.

John's Breathing during Stress Worksheet

1. The phone rings, and I think, "Here we go again." She gets up quickly, and I think, "She'd rather talk to her friends than have dinner with me." I'm sick and tired of eating dinner alone. I can hear her yammering away in the other room. (deep breath)

2. After a small eternity on the phone, she finally comes back. I'm finished eating, and her dinner is cold. I'm not talking. I'm ignoring her. "What's the matter," she says. "You're the matter," I say. "Why do you do this to me every night, make me sit here by myself for dinner?" (deep breath)

3. She goes, "Get off your high horse, I got a life to live too." I can't take that. She'll never admit she does anything wrong. I'm starting to get loud, I'm telling her she's destroying our marriage. She'd better pay some attention to me if she wants to keep me around. (deep breath)

4. She goes, "Thanks for ruining another meal, John. If you had a few friends, maybe you wouldn't be so jealous of mine." That's it. I get up, I grab the stuff off the table, and slam it in the sink. I'm shouting, "This is a nice life, Babe. Thanks for everything." (deep breath)

Putting Stop and Breathe to Use in Your Life

1. Practice Stop and Breathe any time you feel tense for any reason. It doesn't have to be anger. It might just be that you're held up on the freeway, late for work. Or your kids are having a fight over who got the most ice cream. Or you just learned your mother-in-law is coming to visit for two weeks. As soon as you're hit by stress, immediately put a cap on the negative thinking. Remind yourself that you have a choice, that you can choose to relax instead of being stressed. Then do your four diaphragmatic breaths, counting at each exhale.

2. Practice Stop and Breathe with your partner when you're *not* angry. Odd as it sounds, Stop and Breathe becomes most effective if you initially practice it when there's *no* conflict. Make a game of it. Decide in advance that whenever your partner mentions her job, you'll do a round of Stop and Breathe, or every time your partner has to tell you the latest about how the Giants are doing—that's a good time for Stop and Breathe too. Another alternative is to have your partner cue you at random, two or three times throughout an evening, so you can learn to practice Stop and Breathe at unpredictable intervals. The more practice you get during noncombative situations at home, the more likely you'll be able to remember Stop and Breathe when the chips are down and a storm is starting to blow up.

3. Plan in advance for typical anger situations with your partner. If you tend to have fights about household chores, make sure you have a Stop and Breathe plan in place for when things start to escalate. So whether you fight about what you're watching on TV, how to handle Jimmy's homework, or where you're spending your money, try to identify how the fight typically starts. Make a commitment to yourself that you will use Stop and Breathe at a specific point, early enough in the conflict, that will help you gain control of your anger response.

In the space provided below or in your notebook, write down the exact situation and early problem behavior you will use as a cue for employing your new Stop and Breathe skills:

_____

_____

_____

_____

Cue-Controlled Relaxation

Cue-Controlled Relaxation has a miraculous effect on anger. If you use it, it will work. This relaxation technique is so powerful that you can employ it to shut down anger anywhere, anytime. And it takes as little as thirty seconds. You can learn it in two steps. The first is called Progressive Letting Go, and the second is Cue-Controlled Breathing.

Step 1: Progressive Letting Go

To begin with, you'll need a special cue word or phrase that will become your signal to relax. Make it short and authoritative. Some examples might include:

- Relax and let go

- Release

- Breathe and relax

- Calm

- One

- Peace

You can choose your favorite color, or the name of a very peaceful spot. One man used the term "lapis lazuli" to remind him of the famous Yeats poem that defined true peace. Someone we know chose "Tuolomne" as a cue word—after the beautiful meadow in Yosemite.

With your cue word in mind, it's time to learn how to scan and relax the major muscle groups in your body. Use the following sequence to let go of tension:

1. Notice any tension in your lower body—feet, calves, thighs, or buttocks. Now take a deep, diaphragmatic breath. As you exhale, say your cue word or phrase and try to relax away all the tension in your legs. If your legs don't feel completely relaxed, repeat the procedure.

2. Move your attention to your stomach and chest area. Notice any tension in your abdomen, back, or pectoral muscles. Now take another deep, diaphragmatic breath. Say your cue word or phrase as you exhale, and relax away any tension in your chest or abdomen. If you are not completely relaxed, repeat the procedure.

3. Move your focus to your arms and shoulders. Be aware of any tension in your hands, forearms, biceps, or shoulder muscles. Take a deep, diaphragmatic breath. As you exhale, say to yourself your cue word or phrase and relax away tension in your arms and shoulders. If relaxation is not complete, repeat the procedure.

4. Move your awareness to your head. Scan for tension in your scalp, around your eyes, and in your cheeks, jaw, and neck. Take a deep, diaphragmatic breath. As you release the breath, say your cue word or phrase, and relax away any tension in your head and neck. If relaxation is incomplete, repeat the procedure.

Do this Progressive Letting Go procedure as many times as possible over the next three days. Once a day is good, and twice is better, but five or more times a day will really strengthen your relaxation response. What you're doing here is learning to associate your cue word or phrase with that feeling in your muscles when you let go of tension and the release you get from a diaphragmatic breath. The more you practice, the stronger this relationship becomes. After a while, your cue word or phrase by itself will have the power to trigger a relaxation response.

Step 2: Cue-Controlled Breathing

Now we're going to give you the secret of rapid relaxation that can drain away all your anger-generating tension in as little as thirty seconds. It's very simple. You take a deep, diaphragmatic breath. As you exhale, you say to yourself your cue word or phrase, and relax away the tension in your entire body. Try to make all of your muscles feel as relaxed as they did during the Progressive Letting Go exercise that you've just been practicing. Do ten cue-controlled breaths in a row to fully activate the relaxation response. Go ahead and try it right now. Remember not to breathe too fast. Just take a slow, deep breath whenever you need to, use your cue word or phrase as you release the air, and focus on relaxing your body as a whole.

Cue-Controlled Breathing during Stress

To practice this new skill, you can go back to the anger-evoking scene you developed earlier in the chapter. Go through the sequence as before, but instead of doing deep breathing, do two or three cue-controlled breaths. Go through the entire four-step anger scene several times so you become more and more comfortable with Cue-Controlled Breathing during stress.

To master Cue-Controlled Breathing in real-life situations, you can use the same practice steps you used for Stop and Breathe.

1. Practice Cue-Controlled Breathing whenever you feel tense for any reason. It doesn't matter if the tension is triggered by anger or a deadline at work. Just take ten cue-controlled breaths and relax away the stress in your body.

2. Practice Cue-Controlled Breathing with your partner when you're not angry. Ask your partner to signal you at random over the course of an evening to practice your

cue-controlled breaths. Whenever your partner gives the prearranged signal, take your ten cue-controlled breaths. Practicing when you're not angry will make it a lot easier to use Cue-Controlled Breathing during actual conflict situations.

3. Plan in advance to use Cue-Controlled Breathing during predictable conflict situations with your partner. Decide which recurring upset you're going to focus on with Cue-Controlled Breathing, and commit yourself to using it at a particular point in the escalation process. For example, the point where your voice gets loud, when you hear yourself starting to lash out, or when you're mentally preparing some insult. Be very clear on the particular behavior you'll watch for that should trigger Cue-Controlled Breathing. Then do it every time that predictable conflict with your partner flares up.

Eye Movement Technique (EMT)

Sometimes relaxation isn't enough. All the diaphragmatic breathing in the world will not calm certain angry thoughts. You may have noticed how your mind can get stuck in loops, reliving again and again the same upsets and provocations, making judgments about how badly you've been treated, plotting revenge. The more you think these angry thoughts, the more enraged you become; the more enraged you become, the more your mind is aswirl with angry thoughts. It's an escalating spiral that sometimes you may feel helpless to control. Eye movement technique (EMT) is a powerful thought-stopping strategy. It shuts down the loop of angry thinking. It's simple and easy. Here's what you do:

1. Think about a recent situation with your partner that was moderately upsetting. Something that rated about 6 on a 10-point scale of anger. Right now, go ahead and indulge yourself in thoughts about how badly you were treated and how wrong your partner's behavior was. Let it rip; just let yourself get worked up. As soon as your anger reaches a level of about 5 or 6 on that 10-point scale, go to step 2.

2. Run your eyes back and forth from one corner of the room to the other, or spread your legs and run your eyes from one knee to the other. Just make it a smooth motion, back and forth, twenty-five times. In other words, your eyes move from your left knee to your right, and then back to your left knee again. Count one. Each full circuit back and forth gets a count. As you start moving your eyes, don't try to think about anything in particular. Just concentrate on the eye movement experience.

3. When your eyes have completed twenty-five circuits back and forth, stop and evaluate your anger level. Are you still as angry as before, or has your anger dropped? Go ahead and rate it on the 10-point anger scale we've been using. The average person finds that their anger decreases by about 2 or 3 points on the anger scale after using EMT. People also report having difficulty returning to some of their anger thoughts. The images and thoughts seem farther away, harder to generate.

4. Repeat the entire procedure. Crank up your anger thoughts again, trying to reach 6 on the anger scale. When you've gotten as close as you can to 6, let go of the thoughts and begin EMT. After counting twenty-five cycles, evaluate your anger level on the 10-point scale. This time your anger may be even lower. The effects of EMT are additive with each repetition.

5. Repeat the procedure with your eyes closed. You may sometimes be in a situation where you'd be embarrassed using EMT. Learning the eyes-closed version of the procedure allows you to use it any time. You'll just look like you're resting your eyes for a minute.

After three repetitions of EMT, about 70 percent of people report a significant reduction in negative thoughts and images. People say things like, "It just takes the steam out of things." "The thoughts seem a little hard to reach, they don't seem to matter as much." "The thoughts don't make me as angry."

Since your angry thoughts are a big source of blowups, it's important to have a tool to stop them. Every time you notice yourself getting caught up in mental blaming, give yourself a quick dose of EMT. It'll calm down both your thoughts and your angry feelings.

EMT Worksheet

You can use either EMT or Stop and Breathe any time a chain of angry thoughts threatens your calm.

Here's how you get practice. Identify two kinds of angry thoughts that really affect your relationship and write them below or in your notebook. They can include blaming thoughts about one of your partner's faults, angry thoughts about something your partner has already done to you, or attributions about how your partner thinks and feels about you. It doesn't really matter what you choose; it just has to be specific and easily recognizable. In other words, you have to know it when it happens.

Negative Thoughts I'm Going to Watch For

1._____

_____

2._____

_____

Now that you know what you're going to watch for, make a commitment to yourself to use EMT (or if that doesn't work, Stop and Breathe) every time you notice either pattern of thinking. Be serious about this commitment. It'll make a huge difference in your relationship when you can shut off negative thoughts before they incite an outburst.

Tell a friend, or your partner, about this commitment, and ask him or her to help by checking in with you periodically about your progress managing angry thoughts.

What If It Fails?

If relaxation isn't working for you, there are two likely reasons why this may be the case.

1. The first is motivation. Not everyone is prepared to do the necessary work. Monitoring your behavior before an outburst and keeping track of anger-provoking thoughts takes considerable effort. It takes focus and determination. If your motivation so far is tenuous, try to spend some time identifying the negative consequences of anger with your partner. In the space below or in your notebook, write down at least five ways your anger is problematic for you in your relationship.

How Anger Hurts My Relationship

1. _____

2. _____

3. _____

4. _____

5. _____

When you examine these negative consequences, does it give you enough motivation to work harder? Can you recommit to practicing relaxation strategies *during* actual anger events? If the answer is no, this book is not likely to help you. You are encouraged to seek professional counseling.

2. The second major cause of difficulties is that you get so upset you can't remember to use your new skills. Most people have a hard time with this because anger tends to erase everything from your mind. It blows up your best intentions and plans. But you can overcome the problem by employing a reminder to use your coping skills. A simple strategy is to wear something that is unusual and acts as a cue reminding you to stop and cope. A new and unusual ring or piece of jewelry could work, or even an unusual color of nail polish. Sometimes simple things like putting your watch on the other wrist, or putting a sign up on your shaving mirror, can help. You can leave reminders in your wallet, in your desk drawer, or by a light switch.

   If all else fails, ask your partner to help you remember. Tell him or her you're having difficulty remembering your commitment to relax, and would appreciate a reminder *before* the situation gets out of hand. One woman gave her husband a button to wear that read, "Relax, dammit." It worked as a cue for her to cool down. One man programmed his watch to beep every hour as a way to keep his coping plans in mind. It doesn't matter what kind of reminder you use—as long as it works for you.

CHAPTER 3

Understand Your Partner's Feelings

What Is Empathy Training?

Couples who benefit from therapy often report that what helped them most was developing a deeper appreciation for their partner's feelings and experience. The partner ceases to be an adversary. Instead, his or her pain, fear, and past influences are seen and accepted. Rather than focusing on the content of a particular conflict, *Empathy Training* shows you how to recognize and understand eight specific dimensions of your partner's experience. With this new depth of knowledge, anger seems to melt away. You can climb out of the trenches and begin to reach out to each other.

At the heart of Empathy Training is the Couple's Research Form—essentially a structured interview for learning more about your partner. You'll ask your partner questions about each of the key areas, and write down what you learn. Then you'll put this new knowledge to work in an exercise called *Role Reversal*.

The Role Reversal technique is one of many exercises developed by Fritz Perls, father of Gestalt Therapy. The idea is that you play the part of the other person in a conflict, and your partner plays you. During the role play you try to express your partner's feelings, needs, and experience *as if they were your own*. All the information you receive from interviewing and filling out the Couple's Research Form (see page 37) will help you do a better job with Role Reversal—for the simple reason that you now know a lot more about where your partner is coming from.

Where Does It Come From, and Is It Effective?

Empathy Training was developed by the authors in response to research that showed empathy building to be one of the core ingredients of successful couples therapy.

It's very difficult for couples in conflict to understand each other. You're too busy staking out your position, preparing your arguments, and stoking your anger. When you're in conflict, you aren't really interested in your partner's pain, needs, or feelings.

The only way to reverse this process on your own, without the intervention of a therapist, is to commit to a structure—Empathy Training—that forces you to learn more about your partner. You can use the interview format provided in the Couple's Research Form to get below the surface issues and the angry words. You can finally discover the feelings and past experiences that drive and motivate your partner. And your partner can do the same with you. Out of this reciprocal exploration come new opportunities for negotiation and compromise.

In their book, *Getting to Yes*, researchers Roger Fisher and William Ury show that knowledge of the other person's needs and motivations is essential to conflict resolution. We have to stop thinking in terms of winning and losing. Instead, we need to look for outcomes that allow each person to win *because each person's needs, fears, and beliefs were understood and acknowledged in the compromise solution*. If you don't really understand your partner, you'll never be able to do that.

Our clinical experience shows that angry partners who use the Couple's Research Form have marked decreases in anger frequency and increases in solution seeking. Empathy Training builds bridges of understanding that help you focus on mutual solutions rather than prepare for another attack. When you can truly see the world through your partner's eyes, and feel it as though you were in their skin, the whole climate of your relationship changes. The old patterns of anger, driven by seeing things only from your own point of view, will no longer be possible.

How to Use It

The Empathy Training process is something you can do over and over, with any conflict or issue that concerns you. A good problem to start with is one where you've had several fights but no resolution—one where you feel stuck.

To start, you'll each need a copy of the Couple's Research Form (page 37). You can photocopy it or simply write the categories on a sheet (or two) of paper. We suggest writing them out so you can give yourself as much space as you need to fill in your answers. At the top, where it says Issue/Conflict, write a brief, neutral description of the problem. "Sylvia refuses to accept my need for a night out" is not a neutral description. "Bill's lazy-ass lifestyle" is pejorative, and again fails the neutrality criterion. Neutral means you're not blaming or attacking. It means describing the problem in a way both of you can accept. Sometimes the best way to describe a conflict is to label it as the _____ (fill in your own term) issue. For example, "Barbara's schoolwork issue" or "the division of work issue" or "the party issue."

A simple term can stand for a complex problem. For example, "the party issue" is something Art and Lorraine have struggled with for years. Art feels neglected and alone at parties because Lorraine enjoys the get-togethers as an opportunity to catch up with her friends. He complains that she drinks too much. Lorraine moves from group to group, chatting and joking, while Art sips Perrier water in a corner. He also feels threatened because Lorraine is very outgoing with men. The problem has gotten to a point where nearly every social gathering triggers a fight on the way home. "The party issue" is a simple, nonpejorative way to represent this multifaceted conflict.

Once the issue is identified and labeled, it's time to interview each other. Take turns going through the form. Don't judge or criticize your partner's replies. Just repeat back in your own words what was said to make sure you got it right. When your partner confirms that you heard it correctly, write the response down on your form without comment. For the interview to work, your partner has to feel safe with the process. He or she has to feel confident that you won't go on the attack. Remember, you don't have to agree with what's said. You just have to listen, understand, and write it down.

Couple's Research Form

Issue/Conflict:

Needs. What my partner needs or wants:

Fears. What my partner is afraid might happen:

Other Emotional Pain. Other feelings that affect my partner:

History. My partner's experiences from the past (this or other relationships, childhood) that relate to the issue:

Assumptions. My partner's beliefs about the issue, about what will happen in the future, about my motives, feelings, and intentions regarding the issue:

Perceived Choices. What options my partner believes he/she has regarding the issue:

Frame of Mind. What my partner is thinking during the conflict:

Physiological State. What my partner feels physically during the conflict:

Questions to Ask

Here are some example questions to ask for each of the eight sections of the Couple's Research Form:

Needs

- "What would make you feel better?"

- "What specifically would you want to change?"

- "If things could be exactly the way you want them, how would that be?"

- "What do you need to make this work for you?"

- "What's the most important thing you need changed?"

Fears

- "What are you afraid will happen if this situation continues?"

- "When we're in the middle of the conflict, what are you most afraid will happen?"

- "What scares you about this issue?"

- "What's your biggest nightmare of what's going to happen (to you, to me, to us) when this issue comes up?"

- "Has anything happened before that you're afraid will happen again regarding this issue?"

Other Emotional Pain

- "Do you have other feelings that come up in connection to this issue?"

- "Do you feel (hurt, sad, guilty, overwhelmed, ashamed, humiliated, betrayed)?"

- "What's the most difficult feeling that comes up around this issue?"

- "What's the feeling that's hardest to talk about that gets triggered by this issue?"

History

- "Has anything ever happened to you in the past—either between us or even when you were growing up—that affects you regarding this issue?"

- "Are there things you've been through in the past that might influence how you feel or react?"

- "Have you been through anything before that feels like this? With me or in another relationship, or with your family?"

Assumptions

- "What do you believe to be true about this issue?"

- "How do you see this, what's your point of view?"

- "What do you think is going to happen in the future regarding this issue?"

- "Do you think we're headed for trouble? What kind?"

- "How do you see me in this issue?"

- "Do you have ideas about my motives, feelings, intentions, or attitude toward you?"

Perceived Choices

- "What choices do you think you have in this situation?"

- "What options do you think are open? Which ones seem impossible? Which seem too risky?"

Frame of Mind

- "When we're in the middle of the conflict, what are you thinking?"

- "What thoughts are strongest in your mind when this issue comes up?"

- "If I could read your mind when we're struggling with _____, what would I see?"

- "Is there a key thought or idea that usually comes up when this issue is triggered?"

Physiological State

- "What are you feeling physically when we're in the middle of this conflict? How strong is that feeling?"

- "Do you have any feelings in your body when we're in the middle of this issue? Do they bother you?"

Notice that these example questions are neutral, not attacking. They don't assume anything; they don't judge. The underlying message is, "I'm interested in everything you say; any answer is okay."

Example: Jacqueline and Ed

Jacqueline and Ed took turns interviewing each other and filling out the Couple's Research Form around a chronic problem. Ed has a friend named Hanger (because he surfs) who visits at least once a week. Hanger is funny and sarcastic, but also brusque to the point of being rude. Jacqueline has on many occasions felt insulted by Hanger's remarks. She wants Ed to defend her and make Hanger cut it out. When Ed fails to confront his friend, Jacqueline feels betrayed and angry. The issue has triggered dozens of fights. Here are Jacqueline and Ed's completed Couple's Research Forms.

Jacqueline's CRF

Issue/Conflict: Hanger Issue

Needs: Ed needs for me to take care of myself. Stand up to Hanger rationally. Not be hurt or make a fight. Not be upset.

Fears: Ed fears that I'll be angry at him, or that Hanger will be angry at him. Someone will be upset no matter what. He fears the evening that he always looks forward to will be ruined. He's afraid he won't be able to have his friend visit.

Other Emotional Pain: Helplessness, anxiety, anger that he feels forced into a choice.

History: His mother hated Hanger. His ex-girlfriend hated Hanger. Ed is always sticking up for Hanger with people, getting angry at people who insult him.

Assumptions: Ed believes I shouldn't take it personally, that I should deal with it rationally. He believes I'm too sensitive, that I should take care of myself, that I shouldn't force him to choose between his friend and me.

Perceived Choices: Ed sees the choice as rejecting me or rejecting his best friend.

Frame of Mind: "Oh, God, here we go. This is going to end in disaster. Don't do this. I can't stand it."

Physiological State: Sinking feeling, tension

Ed's CRF

Issue/Conflict: Hanger Issue

Needs: Jacqueline wants me to take her side, censor and stop Hanger. She wants me to tell Hanger I won't tolerate his behavior.

Fears: She's afraid I'll be quiet and let Hanger assume it's okay to insult and humiliate her.

Other Emotional Pain: Jacqueline feels humiliated, helpless, and angry when I don't stick up for her.

History: Jacqueline remembers a lot of Hanger's previous insults. In her previous marriage she suffered with someone who ignored her needs. He had affairs with friends of Jacqueline's, disregarding her needs absolutely. Jacqueline also had her needs disregarded by her parents, and by an older sister who never defended or protected her.

Assumptions: She believes that I'm very immature when I'm with Hanger; that all I care about is keeping the good times rolling. Jacqueline believes that I won't protect her, and that I'm offended and embarrassed when she gets hurt by Hanger. She believes that I expect her to just go along and laugh it off.

Perceived Choices: Jacqueline sees a number of choices: putting up with it one night a week, not being around, getting into a fight with Hanger herself, not letting him in the house, being rude to him, trying to get another friend (if they're around) to defend her, or having a fight with me. She seems to think these are all possibilities, but is leaning toward being out on the night Hanger is around.

Frame of Mind: Jacqueline always feels taken by surprise and stunned by Hanger's comments. She believes his behavior is so blatant that anybody who cared about her would step forward and stop it. She believes it must be okay with me for her to be insulted, that her feelings aren't worth anything to me.

Physiological State: Flushed skin, difficulty breathing

Jacqueline and Ed learned a lot about each other's experience through the interview process. Jacqueline was surprised to learn that Ed was so afraid of a scene, and of being rejected himself by Hanger. Ed had had no idea that Jacqueline saw his behavior as an indication that he didn't care about her feelings, or that it was okay with him that she be insulted.

With everything they learned in mind, Ed and Jacqueline decided on a compromise. If Hanger said something insulting, and Ed could see that Jacqueline was upset, he would tell Hanger that the comment had clearly hurt Jacqueline's feelings. He wouldn't label it as an insult, or "get in Hanger's face," but he would tell him that remarks like that hurt Jacqueline. The solution wasn't perfect, but each got some of what they wanted. Jacqueline got Ed to at least acknowledge that a Hanger remark was upsetting to her. Ed got to comment on the situation in such a way that he wasn't directly confronting Hanger and risking a major upset with his friend.

Role Reversal

Now that you've explored each other's experience, it's time for the Role Reversal exercise. Review all the information you wrote down in the Couple's Research Form. Then set an egg timer for ten minutes. During that time you both should talk about the issue, but do so representing the other person's feelings and needs. Try to present them as completely and effectively as possible. Be a good advocate. Explain why you (speaking for your partner) feel so strongly about the issue. Explain the impact of past experiences; explain the beliefs and fears that influence the conflict.

After each person has had a chance to talk, reset the egg timer for another ten minutes. Stay in the role reversal, but this time each of you should offer a compromise solution that somehow addresses *both* partners' needs. A resolution that only takes care of one of you isn't good enough. It will fail in the end because someone's needs have been ignored. Keep talking about your compromise solutions until one of them, a combination of both, or some other alternative feels acceptable to each of you.

Remember that winning is irrelevant. What really matters is agreeing, and finding a way to both feel validated by the outcome.

Example: Reggie and Helena

Reggie and Helena used Role Reversal to work on a conflict about how involved they should be in their thirteen-year-old's homework. Reggie's position was to let her sink or swim. Helena feared that their daughter would get discouraged at school if she wasn't given the support at home to succeed. The role reversal allowed Reggie and Helena to fully explore each other's feelings, needs, and beliefs.

When they reached the compromise phase, Helena suggested that they try it her way one month, and Reggie's way the next, and see how their daughter did with each regime. Reggie suggested getting a tutor to help, but stay less involved themselves. In the end they decided to do both—get a tutor and alternate levels of involvement. They ended the discussion feeling better about the issue than they had in years.

What If It Fails?

If you and your partner both participate, it's unlikely that you'll be disappointed with the outcome. If your partner is reluctant to try the role reversal, you can still practice empathy and try to understand your partner's perspective.

CHAPTER 4

Be Angry
Respectfully

What Is Respectful Anger?

When you're really angry, it's easy to just let it rip and say whatever comes to your mind. Usually that's an attempt to hurt the
other person as badly as they've hurt or are hurting you. You
might not even remember what you say; if you do, you might feel
a little guilty afterward for having said it. But if you're like most
people, you'll assume that whatever you say can later be erased
with the explanation that you were angry. Don't we all say things
when we're angry that we don't mean?

Unfortunately, contrary to the old children's rhyme, "Sticks
and stones may break my bones, but names will never hurt me,"
what you say can often be *more* harmful than a physical blow. In
our experience, people who were verbally abused as children generally say they would prefer to be hit rather than experience the
pain of constant criticism, name-calling, belittling, and other
forms of verbal attack.

When you're angry, you want your partner to stop doing whatever he or she is doing that is causing you pain; you want him or her to back off, to meet *your* needs, to comfort you and make you feel better. But when you lash out, your partner hears only blame and attack, and, like most people, will respond with defensiveness and counterattack. This is where *respectful anger* comes in. Using *I Messages*, you can express yourself and your feelings without attacking your partner. I messages involve taking responsibility for your own feelings and describing what you're experiencing without blame. They leave open the opportunity for respectful problem solving.

Where Does It Come From, and Is It Effective?

It has long been known that pejorative communication erodes not only self-esteem and respect but ultimately the love and trust that are the foundation of any relationship. McKay, Davis, and Fanning (1983) introduced the concept of whole messages. They emphasized that intimate communications must include information about observations, thoughts, feelings, and needs in order for two people to fully understand each other and problem solve effectively. Gottman (1994) described "The Four Horsemen of the Apocalypse," four patterns of negative communication (criticism, contempt, defensiveness, and stonewalling) that lead to marital breakdown. His remedies include using nonblaming I Messages that directly and specifically express feelings without attacking your partner.

When to Use It

I Messages are the foundation of effective negotiation and problem solving. If you're so angry that you can't develop an appropriate I Message, then it's probably better to take a time-out (see chapter 7).

I Messages are useful all the time, and the more you practice when you're not angry, the easier it will be to develop an appropriate statement when you are. Not only is it difficult to think of how to say something that's completely different from what every part of your brain is calling out to say, it's even hard to remember that you're supposed to be thinking of it. A growing feeling of anger and the accompanying realization that your partner is not understanding what you're trying to communicate is one signal that an I Message is necessary. Usually this is the point at which you, like most people, raise your voice and repeat what you've been saying, only louder and more emphatically, perhaps sprinkling in some insults for emphasis ("I can't believe you don't. . . .," "You always. . . .," "You're such a. . . ."). Instead of resolving the problem, this most often leads to retaliation from your partner and a full-scale escalation of conflict.

Another clue that an I Message would be useful is the recognition that although your partner seems to understand what you're saying, he or she hasn't stopped doing whatever painful thing led to the initial conflict. When this happens, it would seem that although the content of your message has been communicated, either the importance of it or your desire to find an alternate path has not come through.

How to Use It

In order for your partner to understand why his or her behavior is hurting you (and therefore stop doing whatever it is that's painful to you), it's essential that you express what you want and need. Effective communication means you maximize your chances of getting your needs met without sacrificing the relationship by ignoring your partner's needs. That means talking in respectful, nonblaming ways, which is really difficult when you're angry. And as you know, when you're experiencing really strong feelings, you can't *not* express yourself. Either you express your feelings directly with words, or you end up acting them out indirectly. Indirect expressions of feeling include silent withdrawal, chilly politeness, sulky passive-aggressiveness, or angry violence.

Example: Marion and Tony

In the following example, you'll see how Tony had to deal with Marion's indirect acting out. Tony arrived at Marion's apartment promptly at 7 P.M. as arranged. He was cheerfully anticipating a pleasant night, not only with Marion, but with two friends from out of town who'd called earlier in the day. Marion had seemed less than enthusiastic when he'd called to check in with her about inviting his buddies to join them, but Tony knew that once she got to know them, Marion would love his friends too.

What Tony didn't know was that inside her apartment, Marion had been stewing since their earlier phone conversation. She hadn't mentioned it on the phone, but she was upset that once again Tony had forgotten that this was their anniversary, and instead of planning a romantic evening for the two of them, had blithely included a couple of strangers (at least to her).

Tony rang the doorbell. Marion composed herself and opened the door. As Tony leaned toward her to give her a kiss and a "Hi doll," she stiffened—only slightly—but enough for Tony to notice. He reacted with puzzlement, "What's up, Mar?" "Nothing," Marion responded coolly as she turned away from him. Tony tried again. "You look really great tonight!" he offered. "Let's go. We'd better not keep your *friends* waiting," Marion answered. Tony shrugged, and as they headed down the steps to the street, he reached for her hand. A second before Tony's hand reached hers, Marion transferred her handbag from one hand to the other, making that hand unavailable to Tony. "What's going on?" Tony demanded, really confused. "What are you talking about?" responded Marion smoothly. "You seem upset about something," Tony ventured. "Really? I'm just fine," said Marion coolly, "There's nothing wrong with *me*." Needless to say, the evening was a disaster.

When you express your feelings indirectly, the resulting behavior is often unclear and poorly understood. Your partner is left to guess exactly what's going on with you, and your needs are left unmet. Because Tony didn't know what was upsetting Marion, there was nothing he could do to remedy it. Furthermore, under these circumstances your behavior is likely to be impulsive, the result of what feels like intolerable pain. These impulses often reflect behavior learned from your family of origin, and because it's learned so early, it's a hard habit to break. But it's a habit that has to be broken—and *can* be broken—in the service of a good relationship.

When you express your feelings and needs directly with words, your partner will have fewer doubts about what you want, and your chances of getting it increase dramatically. When you express yourself effectively, you express yourself respectfully, and your partner doesn't feel attacked or blamed. In the absence of defensiveness, he or she can remain receptive to your needs, and this once again increases the likelihood of your needs being met.

Had Marion used I Messages when Tony called her earlier in the day, their conversation might have been different. Had she expressed her disappointment, they could have negotiated a compromise that left them feeling closer to each other rather than further apart. In the following scenario, that's exactly what happened. Tony called Marion during his lunch hour, knowing that it was typically a slow time for her. "Hi babe!" he said, cheerfully. "Hi Tony!" Marion responded, equally happy to be talking with him. After a couple of pleasantries, Tony said, "Hey Mar, Jody and Liz called—you remember my telling you about them, right? My roommates? Anyway, they're in town and I suggested they join us tonight. What do you think?" There was a pause. "Well," started Marion, taking a deep breath. "It's our anniversary tonight. Of when we met. I was hoping we could have a romantic evening—just the two of us." "Oh doll, I forgot. Is it really our anniversary? Could we do something on our own tomorrow maybe? Jody and Liz are just in town for today," Tony half-apologized, half-wheedled. "I guess so," Marion responded slowly, "but I'm disappointed. I wish you'd remembered it. I was really looking forward to tonight." "I'm sorry Mar," Tony said. "But I really appreciate your doing this for me tonight. I'll make it up to you tomorrow. We'll do the whole shebang: get all dressed up and go for dinner and dancing at one of those romantic slow-dancing joints that you've wanted to go to forever. What do you say?" "Promise?" asked Marion. "I promise," said Tony. "Okay, till tonight then," said Marion. "Love you babe," responded Tony. "Me too," said Marion and hung up, shaking her head in wonder at Tony's boundless enthusiasm for life.

Practicing I Messages

As the example demonstrates, I Messages can transform a situation. An I Message enables you to tell your partner what you see him or her doing, how you feel about it, why you might be reacting to it the way you are, given your personal history, and what you would like from him or her. When you use I Messages, you take responsibility for your feelings without blaming the other person. The feeling statement "I'm feeling lonely and ignored" is far less accusatory than "You never have any time for me." You Messages ("*You* make me furious," "*You* are always so irresponsible about time") blame the other person for your feelings rather than acknowledging that the feelings are your individual response to the other person's behavior ("*I'm* furious," "*I* feel disrespected when you come late to our appointments").

Be wary of the temptation to disguise a You Message in the form of an I message ("I feel that *you* are. . . .," "I feel like *you* always. . . ."). Statements that include "feel like" or "feel that" are usually thoughts or interpretations rather than feelings, and blaming ones at that. It's important to differentiate between your thoughts and your feelings. An I Message does not include thoughts or interpretations about your partner and his or her behavior beyond an explanation of your emotional reaction to it.

To give a complete I Message, you must fill in the following blanks:

When you _____ , **I feel** _____,
           (observation of partner's behavior)   *(your own feeling)*
because _____
           (your interpretation of why you feel the way you do—optional).
I would like _____.
                (your needs or wants)

The first step involves making an observation of the particular behavior that is painful to you. An observation is a neutral statement of fact, like "I just bought a red sweater" or "You're using the umbrella I gave you today." There are no judgments or inferences included in an observation, just the facts. When describing your partner's behavior, avoid inflammatory language. Don't say "When you behave like *such a jerk*," "When you're *so childish*" or "When you act like *a lazy, spoiled princess*." Stick with neutral descriptions of specific behavior, such as "When you criticize me in front of my friends, I feel. . . .," "When you turn on the TV when I suggest we talk about the wedding, I feel. . . .," "When you complain about the restaurant I choose while refusing to offer an alternative choice, I feel. . . ."

Stick with the issue at hand and don't bring up past history. This is not the time to build a case against your partner or bludgeon him or her with a record of past transgressions. Don't say, "I can't believe you didn't remember our anniversary—again," or "In three years you've never remembered a single date that was important to me—not my birthday, not Valentine's Day, not our anniversary." Say "You didn't remember our anniversary." Similarly, a sarcastic or otherwise hostile tone of voice can turn a neutral description into an attack. "You're looking very cool" can mean just the opposite when said sarcastically or in a cold, hostile tone.

When describing your feelings, some of the same rules apply. The feelings part of the I Message must be a neutral statement of fact. You must describe your feelings, not attack with them. "I feel like shit when you. . . ." is inflammatory. "I feel unimportant. . . ." is not. Your tone of voice can turn a neutral message into an attack. When you're really angry, it's tremendously difficult to modulate your tone. Nonetheless it's essential that you remember that a hostile, sarcastic, threatening, or overly loud tone will put your partner on the defensive, making it unlikely that he or she will be able to really hear your message, and thus increasing the chances of a reciprocal attack. Body language signals such as clenched fists, gritted teeth, or hostile glares will have a similar effect. All of which means lessening your chances of getting your needs met.

If you have trouble identifying your feelings, start with the basic question: are they positive or negative? Then explore a little further using the categories glad, mad, sad, and bad. Finally you can begin to explore more sophisticated distinctions of glad (for example, amused, cheerful, comfortable, confident, delighted, excited, fulfilled, happy, joyful, loved, peaceful, playful, proud, relaxed, satisfied, tender, thrilled, wonderful), mad (for example, angry, annoyed, contemptuous, enraged, exasperated, frustrated, furious, hateful, hostile, impatient, irritated, outraged, resentful, touchy, unappreciated, upset), sad (for example, defeated, dejected, depressed, despairing, desperate, devastated, disappointed, discouraged, gloomy, hopeless, melancholy, miserable, pessimistic, resigned, troubled, unloved, worn out, vulnerable), and bad (for example, afraid, anxious, apprehensive, bitter, bored, confused, disgusted, embarrassed, fearful, frantic, guilty, isolated, lonely, overwhelmed, panicky, pressured, put down, terrified, threatened, trapped, victimized).

Some feeling words may be ambiguous and you'll need to add some clarifying words. "I'm really upset" may mean that you're angry, but it also may mean that you're afraid or saddened. "I'm really upset ... I'm furious and hurt," is clear. Finally, ensure that the intensity of your description matches your feelings. Don't say "I'm a little angry" when you're enraged, or "I'm getting frustrated" when you're ready to explode.

The third segment of the I Message, "because," gives you the option of describing why you think you feel as you do. You're under no obligation to explain yourself to your partner at this point, but doing so may provide some useful contextual information. Are your feelings triggered by assumptions you're making about your partner's needs or wants? Are you being reminded of how ignored you felt as a child? Is your partner's behavior triggering memories of a particularly painful experience from the past? Are old feelings of loss and fear being stirred?

Filling in the historical context of "because" reduces the chances your partner will dismiss your feelings and reactions as irrational. Once he or she understands why you're particularly sensitive to certain behavior, your partner will be more likely to experience empathy for your response.

Marion might have told Tony that throughout her childhood her alcoholic father never remembered her birthday, never bought her presents, and often didn't even bother to come home for dinner. Her mother constantly apologized for him and tried to make the day a celebration, but Marion adored her father and his absence both devastated her and reinforced her belief that she wasn't very important.

The fourth and final part of the I Message is the "I would like" part. Here's where you get to say what you want. If you've gotten to this step, you're already ahead of the game, so hang in for the last piece. When making a request of your partner, it's important that you focus on *behavior*. Don't expect your partner to change his or her interests, desires, motivations, or values on request. These characteristics are usually seen as personality traits and not under conscious control. Therefore, "I want you to *want* to spend more time with me, not just do it because I ask you to," doesn't make sense. Indeed, what better reason is there for your partner to do something for you than because he or she knows it will make you happy? A request to change anything other than behavior is likely to be experienced as criticism and elicit defensiveness.

In making a request, focus on observable, specific behavior. It won't help to ask your partner to be "more involved with the kids," "less cold and withholding," or "less critical." More than likely he or she will feel attacked, get defensive, and probably argue that he or she already *is* involved with the kids and by the way, who's calling who critical? Instead, spell out what you mean by "involved" or "critical." "I'd like you to supervise James' homework" is a specific, behavioral request. So is "I'd like you to stop telling the story of my accident when we're out with friends." If possible, describe the desired change in terms of positive behavior rather than negative. That way your partner knows what you'd like him or her to do to replace the negative behavior. "I'd like you to take my hand when we go for walks" gives your partner something more positive to aim for than "I'd like you to stop walking two steps ahead of me."

In order to maximize the chances that your request will be met, stick to one situation and ask for a single change. "I would like you to call me when you're going to be late for dinner, supervise Johnny's homework, take over consulting with the contractors about the kitchen renovation, and start planning a two-week vacation for next summer" is specific and positive, but likely to feel completely overwhelming to your partner and elicit defensiveness and resistance. Any one of those changes alone would be appropriate as a starting point.

Finally, make sure that what you're asking for is reasonably "doable." That means a fair request that isn't going to make your partner feel overly burdened or overwhelmed. "I want you to stop traveling for work" may not be doable. "I would like you to set aside some time each weekend for us to spend together doing something fun and relaxing" is.

Containing yourself when you're itching to pull out all the stops and yell is hard enough. Spending the time thinking through the different components of an I Message and coming up with something appropriate is a challenge. But once you've gathered the four parts, putting it all together is straightforward. When Tony arrived at Marion's house and found her behaving so inexplicably (to him), he might have said to her, "When you turn away from me and won't take my hand (behavior), I feel hurt and confused (feelings). I assume you're angry about something I've done but I don't understand what (explanation of why these feelings are being stimulated). Please tell me what's upsetting you so we can try to fix it (request)." Marion might have responded, "It's our anniversary today—of when we met (observation). When you forget dates that are really important to me and plan an evening with people who are strangers—at least to me (observation)—I feel unimportant and small (feelings). It reminds me of my father never remembering my birthday and how painful that was (explanation of why these feelings are being stimulated). We can't change tonight, but I would like to spend time going through your calendar and writing in some important dates so you're more able to remember them (request)."

Example: Jay and Alex

It was 6 P.M. on a Friday evening. Jay and Alex were getting dressed for an evening out: an annual dinner with Alex's four best friends and their spouses. Alex had been friends with these four women since the kids were in kindergarten together, about eleven years now. Usually they got together without their spouses, and that was just fine with Jay. He didn't enjoy these gatherings—he felt like a fifth wheel, and he didn't really have much in common with the other spouses. Once a year didn't seem like asking too much of him, however, and he hadn't had the nerve to refuse to go. In fact he wasn't sure he'd even told Alex how he felt. Still, he felt out of sorts as he dressed, and Alex's cheerfulness didn't help.

For her part, Alex always enjoyed seeing her friends, especially now that they no longer had the excuse of school-based functions to attend together. They tried once a month to meet over a quick dinner or at least coffee, but lately it had been a bit erratic.

She was excited tonight at the idea of a whole evening to relax over dinner. And with or without Jay, she always had a good time with her friends. She hoped Jay wouldn't drink too much tonight. Usually he limited his alcohol intake to two drinks, but at the last two gatherings of "the clan" he had been somewhat grumpy and definitely drunk by the end of the night. Alex knew that Jay didn't particularly like getting together with her friends. He'd complained once that he'd have enjoyed himself just as much if he'd stayed home watching television, perhaps enjoyed himself even better. But he kept coming each year, and if he were going to come, he could at least stay sober and friendly, she thought. Her friends didn't let it affect the evening, much less their relationship with her, but Alex didn't like the idea of Jay's behavior becoming a predictable nuisance year after year.

Alex glanced over at Jay's set face and sighed. Should she say something or not? Without giving it much more thought, she blurted, "I hope you're not going to get grumpy and drunk again tonight." "What are you talking about?" retorted Jay. "I'm talking about you staggering all over yelling about the perils of big business. That's what I'm talking about," said Alex. "That's crap!" snorted Jay. "I have a few drinks and you're eyeing me like I'm a bloody drunkard." "Well, you certainly acted like one last time," accused Alex. "Yeah? What do you care? You're so busy with your friends you wouldn't notice what I do," responded Jay. Alex was incensed. "If you behaved in a halfway civilized manner, people would be more interested in hanging out with you," she roared.

Jay paused. He knew this path. They both were very familiar with the back-and-forth accusations and counteraccusations that were part of their daily interaction. Maybe this was the time to try the new skill they'd read about in their communication skills book. He looked up at the sign they'd made the previous week and stuck on the bedroom mirror. It read, in capitals, "WHEN YOU (   ) I FEEL (   ) BECAUSE (optional). I WOULD LIKE (   )." Okay, thought Jay. Here I go. What am I feeling? Bad, angry, defensive, he thought. And at dinner how have I felt? Jay asked himself. Ignored and unimportant, he thought. Like a fifth wheel. And hurt too, he added. Why? What is it that Alex is doing that's so awful? She's just hanging out with her friends. Jay played devil's advocate for a moment.

Yes, but she doesn't even acknowledge that I'm there. I don't see the point of going with her if she just ignores me all evening. Does it remind me of anything? he continued. Of course it does, he thought. It feels just like it did when one of Mom's drunkard boyfriends appeared, and she suddenly didn't even acknowledge that I existed. So what do I want? he questioned. I'm not sure, he thought. I guess not to feel ignored and unimportant. No, that's not specific enough. What do I want from Alex? I don't know. I guess I'll try to work that part out with her.

Jay turned to where Alex was sitting at the dresser putting on her makeup, her mouth a rigid line of anger and contempt. He had a moment's hesitation, looking at that mouth. He knew that his temptation to say something like "Why the hell are you so upset, I'm the one you've been insulting all night" was something he needed to resist at all costs. I know that path and it hasn't worked for us all these years, he reminded himself. He took a deep breath to calm himself before speaking. "Alex," he began. "I want to try an I Message from the book." Alex's face briefly registered surprise instead of the contempt that had been painted so vividly there before. She put down her mascara and turned around to face him. "I'm listening," she said roughly. "Okay," said Jay. "When we have dinner with your friends and you spend all your time talking to them, I feel ignored and unimportant. Like a fifth wheel. It reminds me of when Mom's boyfriends would come over and she'd send me outside to play for hours, even at night. It hurts," he added. Jay was shocked to feel the prick of tears behind his eyes, but willed them away. "I would like to not feel that," he continued. "But I'm not sure what would help." He stopped and held his breath while he watched Alex's face and waited for her response.

"Wow," she said. "I didn't realize you felt like that." She paused. "I mean, I knew you thought I ignored you, but I just figured you had the guys to hang out with and that it shouldn't be such a big deal." She paused again. "Wow," she repeated. "I'm so sorry. What can I do? Do you want me to just stay and talk to you?"

Jay almost couldn't believe what was happening. Alex was offering to hang out with him instead of her friends! "Well," he replied, "I don't think I need that. Just come over every now and then and spend a few minutes with me. Or include me in one of your conversations. You know, even just looking over at me and catching my eye would let me know that you're thinking of me, that I haven't ceased to exist for you." "I can do that," Alex said softly. She went over to where Jay stood awkwardly, and gave him a hug. He hugged her back.

After a minute, Alex spoke. "You know, I was so busy getting caught up with my own feelings, I never really thought about what you were feeling. When I would see you pouring yourself yet another drink, I just assumed you were punishing me for asking you to come with me. I felt manipulated, like when my mom used to call me at college and cry over the phone about how I hadn't come home in such a long time. I got good at ignoring her because she was so manipulative. And I guess I ignored you too. I'm sorry." "Well," started Jay, "I hate to admit it, but there probably was some punishing going on. I know when Mom would send me outside I would spend hours dreaming about all the awful things I could do that would make her pay attention to me. I can imagine that on some level I thought that if I got good and drunk you'd notice me. I'm sorry too." After a moment's pause, he continued, "Hey! I think we just passed 'I Messages 101!'" and they both laughed.

What If It Fails?

If your partner responds to your I Message by getting defensive or attacking further, check to make sure that you didn't send a hidden "You" message ("When you behave in this way, I feel like you're just an immature..."). If so, it's essential that you reword it to state your feelings in a clean, nonattacking way. If your I Message was on target, then you need to take the next step and develop a self-care plan.

It's tempting when formulating a self-care alternative to focus on punishing your partner for his or her lack of cooperation in solving the problem. But the focus really needs to be on what you need to do for yourself to take care of the problem rather than to your partner for not helping. For example, if your partner won't help more with household chores, you might choose to forgo your weekly dinner out and use the money to pay for a housecleaner. Or if your partner isn't willing to be more consistently on time, you might choose to take separate cars in order to take care of yourself.

You must keep in mind three rules when developing a self-care alternative:

1. The self-care alternative must be reasonable. Don't use it to make threats of violence or humiliation or of dissolving the relationship. Don't say, "If you can't help me more with the kids' homework then I'm out of here." Instead say, "If you won't help me more with the kids' homework then I will have to use the money we were saving for the vacation to hire a tutor." You're simply letting your partner know what the consequences of not cooperating will be and then allowing him or her to make a sensible decision. Be cautious of overly dramatic ultimatums. Don't say, "If you won't stop working such long hours I'm going to file for divorce." Even if it feels like an appropriate response in the heat of the battle, it's likely to be more problematic in the light of the next morning.

2. The self-care alternative must be specific. Make sure your partner knows exactly what the problem behavior is and what exactly will happen without cooperation. Don't say, "If you don't take care of me better, there'll be trouble." Instead say, "If you aren't willing to spend time talking to me when I get home after work, I'll start spending more evenings with my friends who do listen to me."

3. The self-care alternative must be used consistently. That means that if you say you're going to do something, you have to do it—every time the situation arises. If you don't, then you're simply teaching your partner not to take you seriously or believe what you say. So make sure that your self-care plan is something that you can live with. Don't say, "If you don't come home on time, I won't be here when you do." Instead say, "If you don't call me when you're going to be late, I won't keep dinner for you."

CHAPTER 5

Watch Out for the Four Don'ts

What Are the Four Don'ts?

Research on marital satisfaction has repeatedly shown that over time—especially in the early years—there tends to be a marked decline in marital happiness for both partners (Markman and Hahlweg 1993). Clements, Cordova, Markman, and Laurenceau (1997) reject the hypotheses that marital satisfaction decreases either because couples discover they made bad choices, because they fell out of love, or because they grew apart. Instead they assert that happiness erodes based on the way a couple handles the disagreements and conflict that are a normal part of daily life together. A "relationship bank account" develops that monitors the deposits (positive interactions) and withdrawals (negative interactions) of each partner in the relationship and results in the particular "balance" or level of satisfaction at any time.

There are many kinds of interactions that act as deposits to the relationship bank account, increasing intimacy and satisfaction in a relationship. There are just as many kinds of interaction that act as withdrawals and will over time undermine the success of a relationship. John Gottman (1994) identified four patterns of communication that are so destructive to relationships that he called them "The Four Horsemen of the Apocalypse." For simplicity's sake, we'll call them the *Four Don'ts*. These Four Don'ts are, in increasing order of harmfulness: criticism, contempt, defensiveness, and stonewalling (or withdrawal).

Even in the best relationships, people aren't always content. Complaints—at least occasionally—are inevitable. You're going to do things that your partner doesn't like, and not do things that he or she *would* like you to do. Complaining about your partner's behavior is inevitable. In and of themselves, complaints aren't inherently destructive to a relationship. And although it may not be pleasant or comfortable to do so, you and your partner need to air your dissatisfactions. Making a complaint about a specific behavior is a lot healthier for your relationship than suppressing it. The problem arises when you perceive your complaint is not resulting in the desired change; eventually you may get fed up. Instead of switching to a problem-solving communication style, you may switch to personal criticism. In other words, instead of complaining about your partner's behavior, you condemn him or her personally. Instead of saying "You forgot to take the trash out last night and now we have ants all over," you say, "I can't believe you forgot the trash again. You are so goddamn lazy." Over time, constant criticisms will erode a relationship as surely as water erodes the sand—and just as easily.

Contempt, the second Don't, differs from criticism in that it aims to deliberately insult your partner at his or her most vulnerable points. You know better than anyone how to push your partner's buttons, and you do it with a vengeance. You want to hurt him or her, and for the duration of the fight, you forget that there is anything positive about your partner at all. These interactions rapidly become psychologically abusive.

When the first or the second Don't is established in a relationship, the third is never far behind. No one can tolerate being blamed and criticized for long without responding defensively. Even if you can see that some of the problem you're facing is your responsibility, it's hard to acknowledge that fact if you're feeling attacked or if your partner is not willing to take any responsibility. When criticism and contempt are entrenched, neither one of you is going to be able to do anything but put up defenses against further attack. Defensiveness can involve denying responsibility, making excuses, cross-complaining ("Yeah? Well, you. . . ."), whining, and yes-butting. Unfortunately, defensiveness does nothing to resolve a problem. Instead it makes it worse.

The fourth and most destructive of the Don'ts is stonewalling. This is the point at which you stop listening to your partner altogether and withdraw emotionally from the relationship. When he or she talks to you, you don't react—you just stare in stony silence or shrug with a "whatever you say" look.

Is It Effective?

When a relationship is in trouble, there's usually a reduction in positive interactions between the partners. Typical changes include fewer warm smiles, less cuddling and affection in general, and a decrease in relaxed conversational moments. By increasing the number of positive interactions, you can make deposits in your relationship bank account. However, Gottman and his associates have found that no matter how many deposits of this sort you make, the use of any of the four apocalyptic behaviors will just as surely—and more rapidly—drain your account. Gottman hypothesizes that it takes a ratio of five positive interactions to every one negative interaction just to keep the relationship on level ground. Others (Notarius and Markman 1993) predict that one destructive act can erase even more positive acts, perhaps as many as ten or twenty. Notarius and Markman have shown that the presence of negative behaviors more accurately predicts a relationship's future problems than the absence of positive behaviors.

When you're not angry, it's easier to focus on what you can do to make your relationship better than when you're mad as hell. But it's in the heat of the moment that your efforts really count. Reducing the amount of criticism, contempt, defensiveness, and stonewalling that you engage in will more quickly and effectively put your relationship back on a good footing than any amount of positive intervention.

When to Use It

It's really tough when you've asked your partner time and time again to change something in his or her behavior and nothing changes. It's tempting to start attributing your partner's lack of cooperation to a major character flaw. Nothing seems to work; your partner seems determined to thwart your desires. This is the point at which you may cross the line from complaint into criticism: "I can't believe you forgot this appointment. I just reminded you about it yesterday. You never listen to me!" It's essential to curb the temptation to lash out with generalized, magnified statements about your partner's irresponsibility, laziness, thoughtlessness, etc.

Once criticism makes even a temporary home in your verbal interaction patterns, the drop into contempt is often easily overlooked. From focusing on your partner's personal shortcomings, you allow yourself to become so disgusted with him or her that your contempt drips through into your communications. You begin to use sarcasm and hostility with more frequency, belittling your partner and his or her character. Insults and name-calling show contempt, as do hostile humor and mockery. Your body language might also convey contempt and disrespect through threatening postures or gestures. You may also use contemptuous facial expressions such as sneering, smirking, eye-rolling, and snorting. When you notice that the majority of your thoughts about your partner consist of negative judgments about his or her character, it's time to shift your focus.

Defensiveness is an automatic response to being—or feeling—attacked. When you're angry or hurt, or you're feeling wounded by your partner's allegations of misbehavior, it's hard to avoid getting defensive. Say your partner is demanding that you take responsibility for something, but you're sure it's not yours to take—or at least not all of it. Accepting responsibility for it means that your partner gets away without having to recognize his or her very real (and perhaps very large) part in the picture. So you resist and instead try to persuade your partner to accept his or her part first. Or you make excuses for yourself. Or you point to something your partner has done that is equally negative, for why should you be made to feel bad about something when your partner has done something just as bad and is trying to get off scot-free? At these times, when you're feeling unjustly accused, as if your partner is trying to manipulate you into taking responsibility for something that doesn't seem fair, it's essential that you contain your impulse to retreat into defensiveness and counterattack.

When a pattern of criticism and contempt has set in, you're likely to develop negative assumptions that lead you to anticipate being criticized and attacked during conflict. This anticipation in turn can lead you to react more negatively to what your partner says. The negative assumptions and the inner dialogue surrounding them exacerbate your negative feelings rather than help you calm down. At these times it's easy to get flooded (overwhelmed with strong negative feelings that interfere with your ability to be rational) and be even less able to react calmly to the situation. Over time, the chronic pain of feeling flooded can trigger the desire to withdraw altogether from the relationship.

Stonewalling, a trait more commonly found in men than in women, is the most deadly of all to a relationship. By this time you're close to feeling so emotionally withdrawn that you can't even be bothered to acknowledge your partner's existence, much less the content of what he or she is saying. You've heard it all before, and nothing seems to work to change things between you, so what's the point? The point, of course, is that if you want a relationship, you must be present. You must show up emotionally in order to work through the emotional problems that occur. As tempting as it is to withdraw to the apparent safety of a metaphorical brick wall, it's much more destructive to the relationship in the long term than showing up to the battlegrounds. No one can have a relationship with a wall.

There are several strategies that should be used in combination when trying to avoid the Four Don'ts. Learning how to de-escalate (chapter 6) is essential, while making reparation (chapter 10) will go a long way toward starting the healing. Relaxation skills (chapter 2) are important for calming down when you're feeling attacked or upset, while calling Time Out (chapter 7) is also necessary when you're unable to respond to the situation appropriately without escalating. Changing how you think about your partner (chapter 3) helps decrease your level of distress. When you're calm, I Messages (chapter 4) and Negotiation (chapter 7) provide the necessary tools to help you approach solving the problem.

How to Use It

The first step in halting the slide from complaints to criticism is to understand the difference. How does a complaint differ from a criticism? A complaint is any kind of statement that describes your displeasure in your partner's behavior. "I didn't like the message you left me today. You sounded impatient" is a complaint. So is "You forgot to buy milk today." A criticism is a statement that attacks your partner's character, such as "You had your typical shitty tone of voice again" or "You forgot to buy the milk today—as usual." A complaint can easily turn into a criticism when you let your frustration direct the tone of your statement ("I've made this complaint a million times and nothing changes") or when you imply that your partner knows (or should know) how his or her behavior affects you and is doing it anyway.

In order to refrain from criticizing your partner, use I Messages to describe exactly what your partner is doing that you find upsetting, and negotiation skills to combat whatever ongoing problem has not been resolved by repeated complaints. "I'm disappointed that you forgot to buy the milk today. The kids won't be able to have cereal in the morning unless one of us goes out tonight to buy some" is an I Message that is also a complaint. "Since you agreed to do the shopping, I'd like to talk about how we can make it easier for you to remember to buy the milk when we need it" is an invitation to problem solve.

In order to refrain from using contempt, you need to remember that you and your partner are on the same team and that deliberately hurting him or her will actually hurt you as well. When you're not angry with your partner, remind yourself of the reasons why you love, admire, and respect him or her. Respect is a great antidote to contempt. Also, develop some coping statements such as "I can cope without blowing up" or "We're still on the same team, even if I'm mad," and repeat them to yourself frequently. Take some deep breaths and practice the relaxation skills from chapter 2. Then formulate your response using an I Message (chapter 4). I Messages express directly how you feel about a specific situation without blaming or criticizing your partner's personality. They don't include mocking, insulting, or sarcastic language. Pay attention to your body language. Contempt can be as easily communicated nonverbally as verbally.

Defensiveness is the flip side of contempt. After your complaints have gone unheeded, your level of frustration grows, and before you know it you're responding to your partner with sarcasm and hostility. This is how contempt becomes part of your relationship. On the flip side, when your experience is of repeated complaints and criticism from your partner, it's easy to get defensive as his or her complaints become more pointed criticisms and personal attacks. Just as the impulse to use contempt can be contained by reminding yourself why you respect your partner, that you're on the same team, and that you have some relaxation skills and communication skills that can help you, so too can the impulse to become defensive be contained. Once you curb the impulse, it's important to try to listen to your partner's complaints and address them using I Messages to formulate your response. Acknowledging your responsibility for behaving in a way that upset your partner—or better still, apologizing for it—can go a long way toward repairing a troubled relationship.

As mentioned earlier, Gottman's theory is that stonewalling, or withdrawal, is the most deadly of the Don'ts. In this behavior pattern, you simply stop responding to your partner's complaints or criticisms. You might look straight through your partner with a stony-faced stare, or you might not even bother to look up from what you're doing. The message you convey to your partner when you stonewall is that what he or she is saying—indeed his or her very existence—is meaningless to you at this moment. Although you might think that by stonewalling you are preventing further escalation of conflict, the actual effect of stonewalling is usually to provoke your partner to ever-increasing attempts to wring a response out of you. Far from being a "neutral" response, it communicates hostility and disrespect.

Gottman (1994) found that for the most part men stonewall more than women, and that women are more upset physiologically by their partners stonewalling than men are when their partners stonewall. Since men tend to get flooded more easily by conflict than do women, it makes sense that men would see stonewalling as a useful strategy to avoid increasing feelings of being overwhelmed. But stonewalling implies that you're not even listening, that the relationship and its problems aren't worth attending to. So it also makes sense that women would react with escalating outrage and increasing demands for attention and a response.

To avoid stonewalling, it's essential that you give your partner at least the minimal signs that you are listening. Nodding your head and occasionally saying "Uh-huh" or "Yeah" are ways of indicating that you are participating in the interaction, that you want to be present in your relationship. It's important that your facial expressions don't convey withdrawal either. Don't roll your eyes or sneer while your partner is talking. Beware of using a hostile stare or belligerent posture to interfere with communication.

The most important tool for containing the temptation to stonewall is to be able to soothe yourself when you start to feel flooded. In order to do that, you must practice the relaxation and calming exercises described in chapter 2. Practicing them when you're not angry or upset will make it easier to remember to use them when you are. Repeated practice will also make your body more responsive to the exercises once you remember to use them. You also need to practice the strategies for calming your negative thoughts since they too are responsible for triggering flooding. Repeated practice of self-calming thoughts will also make them more available when they are really needed—in the middle of a conflict.

Example: Daphne and Chris

Daphne and Chris had been married twelve years and had two daughters, both in elementary school. When they met, Chris was the attorney for a big engineering firm, Daphne a part-time dental assistant. In their first year of marriage Chris convinced Daphne to quit her job, do volunteer work, and eventually be a stay-at-home mom. Daphne reluctantly agreed, and for four years their home life was comfortable and relatively stress free. Then the firm Chris worked for was bought by another engineering company and in the resulting reorganization Chris was laid off. Suddenly their lives were turned upside down.

After almost six months of looking, Chris accepted a job with a small group of attorneys at a greatly reduced starting salary. It was clear to both of them that Daphne would need to go back to work. Unfortunately, after four years she was out of touch with the dental field and could only find a job doing unskilled retail work. After-school care needed to be arranged for the girls, and by the time everyone got home at night, the level of exhaustion was overwhelming.

It wasn't long before Chris started complaining about the state of the house. It never seemed to be clean anymore. Gradually his complaints grew to incorporate the fact that he never seemed to have any clean shirts, dinner was never ready on time, and the bills didn't seem to get paid when due. Daphne, for her part, complained that since she now worked full-time, she couldn't manage all the household responsibilities alone, and that Chris should be taking on some of them himself. Chris already felt demeaned by the whole experience of being laid off and having to take such a huge salary cut. There was no way he was going to take on the chores that "belonged" to Daphne.

Nothing improved in the months that followed. Chris continued to make subtle and not-so-subtle complaints about the state of the house. Eventually his complaints became more personal criticisms. Daphne felt more and more overwhelmed, trying to juggle the responsibilities of work, kids, and home. She felt blamed and unsupported by Chris, and furious that he just assumed that she would take care of everything—as she had when she was not working outside the home. The interactions that characterized their evenings were hostile and critical. All four Horsemen of the Apocalypse were at home in their living room.

On this particular night Daphne got home with the kids at 6:30. Chris arrived at 6:45. Both were exhausted. "Great, dinner's not ready again—what a surprise," Chris muttered as he hung up his coat and saw the chaos spread over the dining room table. "What a pigsty!" he added in a slightly louder, contemptuous voice. Daphne was just coming out of the kitchen. "Well, if you weren't so *lazy* maybe it wouldn't look this way," she sniped defensively. "Well, if you weren't such a *slob* it wouldn't get this way in the first place," he shot back. "Oh right!" sneered Daphne, "I forgot. You don't contribute to any mess in the house. That's why you don't have to help with anything. You're so wonderful you don't have to eat, your clothes don't get dirty, you don't run up any bills, you're just Mr. Perfect. And you're sure bringing in a perfect salary, aren't you? Well, if you want to eat, Mr. Perfect, you're going to have to do some work for it and help clear the table." Chris' gaze had become stony and blank during Daphne's diatribe. As Daphne slowed down to take a breath, Chris turned on his heel and walked out of the room. His heart was pounding and he felt flooded with rage and anxiety. All he could think of was to get away, and he headed to the den to watch the news.

To Chris' dismay, Daphne followed him. "Well, do you want to eat or not?" she persisted. Chris said nothing. He turned on the television and sat down, staring at the screen. "Well, that's polite," Daphne began. "Just walk away and refuse to answer. Typical. When it's something you don't want to hear, you think you can just shut me out and everything will be fine," she continued. "Well, it won't." Chris jumped up from the couch and lunged from the room. He tore his coat off the hook and slammed the front door behind him as he left. Daphne ate dinner silently with her two girls that night. Chris didn't return till well after midnight. Daphne was already asleep.

Three weeks later Daphne and Chris talked about the state of their marriage. Daphne had read some books about communication and had left them on the table, hoping Chris would read them. He hadn't, but he was willing to talk with Daphne because he could see that if things continued the way they were, their marriage was headed quickly for the rocks. Neither Daphne nor Chris was terribly optimistic, but they both committed themselves to trying to improve their relationship one more time. Over the next few days they studied and practiced I Messages and listened to the relaxation tapes Daphne had bought. Daphne printed up some signs that read:

NO CRITICISM

CONTEMPT

DEFENSIVENESS

STONEWALLING

She stuck one each on the bedroom mirror, behind the bathroom door, and on the fridge.

It wasn't long before they had the opportunity to try their new skills. Chris arrived home one evening to find the house dark and empty. He turned on the lights, turned up the heat, and walked to the kitchen to see if Daphne had left him a note on the table. Nothing. He started angrily toward the fridge to check for leftovers when he saw the sign posted on the fridge door: NO CRITICISM, CONTEMPT, DEFENSIVENESS, STONEWALLING. At the same time he heard the front door open and the cheerful chattering of Daphne and their daughters. His mind racing, trying to formulate the right I Message, Chris blurted out in a somewhat aggrieved tone of voice, "I wish you'd let me know when you're going to be late" as the three walked into the kitchen and laid down their packages. Even though Chris had tried to refrain from criticizing, Daphne was instantly defensive. "You mean because *you* always call when *you're* going to be late?" she began sarcastically. For a moment Chris felt a tremendous impulse to spin on his heel and march back to the den and the news. He felt safe in front of the television where he could tune out Daphne's attacks more easily—if temporarily. He looked back at the sign on the fridge. NO STONEWALLING. He resisted the impulse to withdraw and tried to think of what to say. Meanwhile, Daphne's eyes had followed Chris' to the sign she had stuck to the fridge, and she paused. "Sorry," she apologized. Then in a calm voice she continued, "We were held up by an accident on the freeway. I had planned to be home long before this. Otherwise I would have left you a message." In her head Daphne reminded herself of the phrases she had chosen as her mantras to help her combat her defensiveness: "We're on the same team, he works hard for us, and he's a great dad." She sighed and began pulling things out of the fridge to prepare dinner.

Meanwhile, the girls had started unpacking their bags and now showed Chris their purchases before heading upstairs to put them away. Each had a new dress, a sweater, and pair of shoes. As soon as the girls were out of earshot Chris blurted, "What the hell were you doing today? Trying to bankrupt us?" "Look," Daphne began, patiently trying to ignore the critical note in Chris' voice, "it's the girls' violin performance next week and they really wanted something to wear besides their regular school clothes. Besides, I got a bonus today for having made the most sales this quarter! We were sort of celebrating." Chris was embarrassed by having fallen so quickly back into old patterns, especially with Daphne's sign only inches from his face. His embarrassment was painful to him and he felt defensive: "Well, thanks for celebrating with *me*," he wanted to grumble. Instead he reminded himself of his chosen mantra: "We both really want what's best for the family," and congratulated her.

Dinner was relatively pleasant, if a little subdued, and later in bed, Daphne congratulated them on their successes. "We weren't perfect, but we weren't screaming at each other either!" she praised. "And you didn't run away to watch television when I slipped back into getting defensive! That was great!" she added with a smile. Chris looked at Daphne's face, lit up with both pride and gratitude. He didn't often get the chance to notice how lovely she looked when she smiled, and he smiled back. It was a small step toward repairing their marriage, but it felt great.

What If It Fails?

The strategies described above to help prevent the Four Don'ts from destroying your relationship are only useful if you remember them. You no doubt lead a busy life full of work and family responsibilities; remembering to practice relaxation strategies, cognitive mantras, or positive thoughts about your partner can be problematic. However, the only way to decrease these negative influences is through practice, practice, and more practice. *Overlearning* is the name given to the process of learning a skill so well that it becomes almost second nature. By overlearning these strategies, you'll increase your chances of remembering to use them when you need them most: when you're really angry.

If despite all your practicing you find yourself responding with one of the Four Don'ts, don't despair. Just try again. Call a time-out (see chapter 7), and take the time to relax and cool down. Formulate an I Message and ensure that your nonverbal communication is consistent with what you're saying verbally.

It's also important to remember that you don't need perfection to have a good relationship. Between every couple there are complaints and occasional criticisms. It's the regular, entrenched nature of the negative interactions that does the most damage. When your automatic reaction to your partner is to make a personal criticism, a contemptuous retort or to simply stonewall and retreat behind a wall of silence, you know you're in trouble.

CHAPTER 6

Learn to De-Escalate

What Is De-Escalation?

If you struggle with anger, you probably "find" yourself sniping at your partner, yelling, or engaging in a chilly silence. Once you've reached that state, or when you suddenly realize you're headed down that slippery slope, it's difficult to turn the interaction around. Psychologist John Gottman (1994) developed a "repair checklist" to facilitate the process of *de-escalating* marital conflicts. This repair checklist is a list of phrases that can help repair an already-damaging interaction. A partner's use of the checklist indicates a desire to shift from the negativity and hostility that might characterize your usual interactions, toward something more relationship-enhancing. These attempts at repairing a damaging interaction include statements of feelings (i.e., "I'm feeling defensive, can you rephrase that in a gentler manner?"), of apology ("I'm sorry, how can I make things better?"), of appreciation ("I know this isn't your fault"), and of agreement ("I think your point of view makes sense"); requests for a pause in the discussion ("I'm feeling flooded, let's take a break"); and requests that your partner help you calm down ("Please help me calm down").

Another strategy for de-escalating conflict is to find something in what your partner is requesting or saying that you can understand and comply with. This doesn't mean agreeing with everything your partner is saying, nor blindly putting aside your own needs for those of your partner. But it communicates to your partner a desire to find a middle ground between your position and his or hers. Gottman called this strategy "accepting influence." The key belief behind the success of accepting influence is that when one or the other of you wins, the relationship loses, and that when you can find a way to compromise, the relationship wins.

Where Does It Come From, and Is It Effective?

Gottman developed his repair checklist as a tool to help couples de-escalate their conflicts. He found that it works best when the receiver commits to trying to accept the repair attempt as such. That means the receiver must accept influence, by finding the part of the repair attempt that he or she can agree with and accept for now.

Repair attempts achieve two things. First, they communicate to your partner that you're aware that things are getting heated and that you'd like to get them back on track. Secondly, they shift focus from the content of the conflict to the relationship, allowing the health of the relationship to become top priority.

When to Use It

De-escalation strategies are best used before your anger gets out of control. By now the pattern of your fights is probably quite familiar to you. As soon as you recognize that pattern, and see that the conflict between you and your partner is going to escalate, you can begin to use repair attempts. Alerting your partner to your attempt will make it easier for him or her to accept the attempt and further de-escalate.

How to Use It

The first step in de-escalating is to develop your repair checklist. In a journal or notebook, copy the following lists. After the sample statements, write at least six more statements in each of the categories. Use the sample statements to guide you. Try to develop the checklist together with your partner if possible. You can write each statement together or each come up with a few of your own. When you've finished writing at least six statements for each category, make two copies, one for each of you.

Repair Checklist

I'm Feeling

1. I feel misunderstood.

2. That really hurt my feelings. Can you say it differently?

3. I'm feeling criticized.

4.

5.

6.

7.

8.

9.

I'm Sorry

1. That didn't come out right. Let me try again.

2. I'm getting too loud. Sorry.

3. I can see how I'm making this hard. I'm sorry.

4.

5.

6.

7.

8.

9.

I Need to Calm Down

1. I need your help in calming down right now.

2. Can we just be quiet together for a minute?

3. Could you be gentler with me please?

4.

5.

6.

7.

8.

9.

I Need to Stop

1. I need to stop for a while.

2. Please let's take five.

3. I'd like to agree to disagree about this.

4.

5.

6.

7.

8.

9.

I'd Like to Compromise

1. I can really see your point.

2. I'd like to find some common ground.

3. I think we could compromise.

4.

5.

6.

7.

8.

9.

I Appreciate

1. Thank you for hanging in with me.

2. I really appreciate what you're saying.

3. I understand that this really isn't your fault.

4.

5.

6.

7.

8.

9.

When you and your partner have developed a repair check-list, it's time to practice using it. Decide together on a topic to discuss, preferably not one that you have had endless trouble resolving. Make sure the issue is framed without blame, i.e., "Tom's work responsibilities" rather than "Why Tom's a wuss with his boss" or "Jennifer's little attitude problem." Give yourselves fifteen minutes to discuss the selected issue.

Once you begin the discussion, pay close attention to your physical and emotional state. Watch for signs of tension or anxiety: clenched fists, a tightening of the jaw or forehead, a raised voice, or any other precursor of anger that signals potential escalation of the discussion into argument. Watch your partner's facial expression and body language for similar signs of tension or anger. At the earliest sign of escalation, either in yourself or your partner, turn to your checklist. Decide which of the six categories fits your situation best. Do you want to express what you're feeling, apologize for your part in the potential escalation, take some time to calm down or take a break, find a compromise, or let your partner know you appreciate him or her? When you've decided which category fits best, look through the list for the phrase that fits. Tell your partner which repair attempt you're going to use by declaring, "I'm making a repair attempt. It's category "I'm sorry," number 4," before reading out that statement (i.e., "I'd like to make things better. Can I say that again in a different way?"). It's very important that you alert your partner to your repair attempt so that the attempt doesn't get overlooked or misinterpreted.

If you're the partner receiving the repair attempt, it's your job now to accept that attempt and continue de-escalating. When your partner alerts you to the fact that he or she is going to use a repair statement, you have time to prepare your reaction. Without this preparation, it's easy to automatically discount the attempt and respond with something that further escalates, like "Oh sure, *now* you want to make things better because you see that I'm right." With your partner's warning, you have time to remind yourself that his or her interruption of the discussion is an attempt to make things better. Find a part of the repair statement that you can agree with (accepting influence) and state your agreement, for example "Yes please, it'd be great if you'd say that again."

Accepting influence in the service of de-escalation is a useful strategy in conjunction with your repair checklist. However, it is also a powerful strategy when used alone. At the earliest sign of escalation between you and your partner, take a breath and think about what your partner has just said to or asked of you. Is there something in your partner's statement or request that you can understand and accept? Something you can agree with? Find the part that makes sense to you, however small, and express your understanding and agreement to your partner. Assume your partner calls and tells you that she has to meet with some really important clients tonight and asks if you would pick up the kids. Instead of responding, "Why should I jeopardize my career to pick up the kids tonight? We agreed that that's your job," try "I understand that your meeting tonight is very important but I don't feel comfortable leaving work early. How about I call my sister and have her pick them up?"

Accepting influence doesn't mean acquiescing without question, or completely putting aside your own needs. It simply means finding a part—however small—of your partner's request or position that you can agree with, and going from there. The message to your partner is that you recognize that for the relationship to win, his or her needs have to be respected and included along with yours.

Example: Myron and Londa

Myron's mother wanted to visit over spring break and Myron knew it wasn't going to be easy. Her visits—even the anticipation of them—inevitably caused tremendous conflict between him and Londa, and this visit was no exception. From the moment he'd mentioned it to Londa, she'd been angry and hostile, and they'd ended up screaming at each other. The difference this time was that they realized what was happening—and they decided to try something new.

That evening Myron and Londa got together with a pen and six pieces of paper to develop a repair checklist. At the top of each piece of paper Myron wrote one of the six headings: I'm Feeling, I'm Sorry, I Need to Calm Down, I Need to Stop, I'd Like to Compromise, and I Appreciate. Over the next hour he and Londa came up with the following lists of repair phrases.

Myron and Londa's Repair Checklist

I'm Feeling

1. I'm feeling blamed for all this.

2. I'm starting to get really anxious.

3. I don't know exactly what I'm feeling, but it doesn't feel good.

4. I feel very unloved right now.

5. This is very painful for me.

6. I don't feel heard.

I'm Sorry

1. I didn't mean to use that tone of voice, I'm sorry.

2. That was a jab, sorry.

3. Let's start all over again.

4. I can hear myself getting shrill. Sorry.

5. I'm being unfair, sorry.

6. I haven't been listening to you at all. Sorry.

I Need to Calm Down

1. I feel overwhelmed and need time to calm down.

2. I need to take a few deep breaths right now.

3. Please give me a minute to calm down.

4. I can't think straight right now.

5. I'm feeling too agitated to talk for a few minutes.

I Need to Stop

1. Let's talk about something else for a while.

2. I need to take a break.

3. Let's put this on temporary hold.

4. I need a time-out for a few minutes.

5. I'd like to get back on track.

6. Let's move on from here.

I'd Like to Compromise

1. What you're saying does make sense.

2. I understand what you're saying.

3. I don't think we're too far apart here.

4. That's a really good point.

5. I hadn't thought of that before.

6. I hadn't looked at it that way before.

7. I can see why you'd say that.

8. I think I can agree with what you're saying.

I Appreciate

1. I'm grateful you're not raising your voice.

2. Thanks for not walking away.

3. I'm glad we're in this together.

4. I appreciate that you're not giving up on me.

5. Thanks for working on this with me.

6. I know this is my issue, thanks for helping me.

To the bottom of each of the six lists, they added the three example phrases listed in the first "Repair Checklist" example. Then they made two copies, one for each of them.

The following night—with lists in hand—they were ready to talk about Myron's mother's impending visit. Myron, already feeling somewhat defensive, began, "I know you don't like my mother, but I thought this would be a good time for the kids to spend some time with her, and she could help you out with them so you wouldn't have to take the whole week off work." "I don't dislike your mother," responded Londa, "but her 'helping' means sitting around telling me what I should be doing better, and why our kids aren't as good as you were. Believe me, that's no help. It's a tough enough week just trying to juggle the kids and work. If you want her to come badly enough, *you* should take the time off work." "You know I can't take time off work, honey," Myron began, but Londa interrupted him. "Don't 'honey' me. What makes your job so damned important compared to mine? I'm the one making the most money."

Myron heard Londa's voice getting shrill and felt his own jaw tighten. He remembered his list and looked it over. "I'm making a repair attempt," he said, "from category 'I'm Feeling,' number 1. I'm feeling blamed for all this." Londa looked at him with curiosity. She'd already forgotten about the repair checklist. She knew it was her job now to find a part of what Myron said that she could accept and agree with (accept influence). "I guess I am blaming you. It's your mother and you want her to come," she tried. "I meant far more than that," started Myron. "Never mind. I didn't realize my mother was so difficult to be around," he continued. "I wish you'd told me sooner." Londa exploded, "I can't believe you're saying that! Why do you think her visits cause so much trouble? I'm constantly trying to tell you and you never listen to me! It's just another example of. . . ." But as Londa glared at Myron, she saw his eyes flicker toward his copy of the repair checklist again, and her criticism trailed off. "Okay, okay" she said with a tight smile. "I'm making a repair attempt. I guess it had better be from category 'I'm Sorry'. . . let's see . . . number . . . well, a lot of them fit . . . maybe numbers 2 and 4. That was a jab and I can hear myself getting shrill. Sorry." "Thanks," said Myron. "And look, you're right. I *have* heard you say things about my mother before. I guess I haven't wanted to hear them. What if instead of coming for the whole week she comes on Thursday night and stays the weekend? Then you only have to deal with her for one day on your own. On the weekend she and I can take the kids out and you can have some time on your own?" "Now *that* I can deal with," said Londa. "If your mother is willing to come for just three days, that would be great." "She will be," assured Myron. "She'll be miffed, but she'll come. And hey, I appreciate your willingness to work on this with me." "Hey," teased Londa, "That's not on the list!"

What If It Fails?

The success of these strategies depends on your willingness to accept that you can either win or have a good relationship, but not both. When you're on a roll and finally driving your point home to your partner, that's when you're probably doing the most damage to your relationship. That's the moment where you have to be willing to stop, back off, and see what you can accept of your partner's perspective. It's not easy.

Ensure that you give your partner notice that you're making a repair attempt, and that your tone of voice when giving your repair statement is consistent with wanting to put the relationship first. Eliminate any unwelcome tones of sarcasm or contempt. Commit to responding to your partner's repair attempt with an attempt to accept influence. It may not be easy, but neither is living in an endless battle zone where, with every individual "victory," the relationship suffers a major defeat.

CHAPTER 7

Try Time Out and Negotiation

The two strategies we'll discuss in this chapter are inherently linked. *Time Out* will enable you to call a halt to a painful interaction before it becomes irreparably destructive to your relationship. *Negotiation* will allow you to discuss the issues on your return calmly and respectfully, reducing the need for further time-outs. Because these separate concepts work so well together, they are presented in tandem in this chapter.

What Is Time Out?

When you're really angry, it often seems that no matter what you say, you're going to end up attacking or feeling attacked. You probably know what it's like to be so angry that you don't even care about the consequences of what you say or do. Time Out is a structured method for helping you stop before you get to the point where what you say might irreparably damage the relationship. It provides time to cool off, as well as a way to return and check in with each other, giving yourselves another chance to address the hot topic. When one of you calls a time-out, all inter-action has to immediately stop. You then separate for an hour and engage in some cooling-down behavior alone. When the hour is up, you return and try again to discuss the topic.

Where Does It Come From, and Is It Effective?

Daniel Sonkin was one of the pioneers of the Time Out procedure (Sonkin and Durphy 1985, 1997). As a psychotherapist working with domestic violence cases in the San Francisco Bay Area, he recognized that anger management treatment helped to avert reoffenses with many of the court-mandated cases he treated in groups. Sonkin's work was adapted by Jeanie Deschner in her book *The Hitting Habit* (1984) into the Time-Out Contract below.

The rationale of a time-out is simple: If you can't talk about a problem without the discussion turning into a fight, it's better not to talk about it. A time-out provides the structure to end a danger-ous escalation as well as the opportunity to return to the problem and attempt to solve it with less anger. When used properly, before things get out of hand, it is extremely effective. Even when a conflict has escalated, a time-out can effectively stop the situa-tion from deteriorating further.

When to Use It

When you're in the middle of a conflict, it's hard to stop. Once you're feeling so hurt or misunderstood or attacked that the launching of your own counterattack feels inevitable, even think-ing of calling a time-out may be unrealistic. A time-out is there-fore most effective early in the interaction when you first recognize the familiar signs or patterns of escalation that you know lead nowhere but trouble. You might notice that you're clenching your fists—which often leads to punching a hole in the wall. It might be that you hear your voice getting loud and shrill. You might become aware of feeling frightened or anxious. It might be the point where you just want to punish your partner.

As soon as your emotions get really heated, your ability to problem solve decreases. Some people only recognize high levels of anger, those that would score above 5 on a scale of 1 to 10. They miss the signs of frustration and irritation that usually precede full-scale anger. If you're one of those people, it's important that you pay close attention to the physiological cues that go along with early anger, from tension in your jaw or neck to knots in your stomach. These are the signals for you to call a time-out.

Relaxation and calming exercises (see chapter 2) can be used during the cooling-down phase of a time-out. When one of you has called a time-out, you agree to separate for an hour. During that time, your task is to calm down, and relaxation exercises are an effective means for doing this.

How to Use It

There are four steps to a time-out:

1. A time-out is communicated simply and effectively by using the same "T" sign that referees use during sports matches. The "T" sign, made with the hands, can be enough, without any accompanying words other than "Time-out!" That's the signal for you (or your partner) to stop talking and return the gesture. It's okay to say "Okay, time-out"—but don't say more than that. You might be tempted to say, "I can't talk to you anymore, let's have a time-out," "You're driving me crazy, I need time away," or "You're completely out of control." But such remarks will only make things worse, not better. Calling for a time-out using blaming language will increase your partner's defensive feelings and lead to further escalation. This isn't the time to get the last word in, either. No explanations, no last rebuttals, no finishing a thought. The "T" sign, once made, must end all further discussion between you.

2. Whoever calls the time-out should immediately leave the room, or, ideally, the house. It's helpful to decide ahead of time where each of you will go for this agreed-upon separation. A time-out of one hour provides a good cooling-off

period, while reducing the chances that either of you will feel abandoned. While it's essential to have enough time to cool down, it's even more important to return at the end of the hour. Although it's hard to return to an unresolved conflict without the protection of anger, not coming back will only make things worse. The partner who leaves *must* return on time; the one remaining at home *must* be available at the appointed hour.

3. Once you've separated, your task is to calm down. Doing something physically challenging is often the best choice. Go for a walk or run or swim; ride your bike or scooter; sweep the floor or clean the garage. Physical challenges can reduce the tension in your body as effectively as relaxation or calming exercises. Even better is some combination of the two: as you exercise, notice any angry thoughts that arise, but don't hang on to them. Let them float away down a river in your imagination. Remind yourself that your task is to de-escalate, not to build your case or rehearse angry responses in readiness for your return. Don't visit friends who'll encourage you to talk about the conflict and side with you, adding fuel to your fire. Stay away from drugs and alcohol, and in the interests of your safety and that of others, stay off the road and don't drive.

4. At the end of one hour, it's essential to check in with each other. Ask if your partner is ready to talk about the conflict. If you're still upset and unable to talk calmly, set a specific time to reexplore the issue, so that it doesn't get swept under the rug. If you're able to talk, ensure that you follow the rules for respectful negotiation, which you'll learn later in this chapter.

The Time-Out Contract is a useful tool to help solidify your commitment to the procedure. It's easier to take things seriously when they're in writing. Use the contract offered here (adapted from Deschner 1984) as a framework to help you remember what's at stake.

Time-Out Contract

When I realize that my (or my partner's) anger is rising, I will give a "T" signal for time out and leave at once. I will not hit or kick anything, and I will not slam the door.

I will return no more than one hour later. I will take a walk or use up the anger energy and will not drink or use drugs when I am away. I will try not to focus on resentments. When I return, I will check in to find out if my partner is ready to resume discussion. If not, we will agree on a specific time to reexamine the conflict.

If my partner gives a "T" signal and leaves, I will return the sign and let my partner go without a hassle, no matter what is going on. I will not drink or use drugs while my partner is away, and I will avoid focusing on resentments. When my partner returns, we will resume discussion or set a specific time for reexamining the conflict.

Name: _____ Date: _____

Name: _____ Date: _____

Practice, Practice, Practice

It's impossible to overemphasize the importance of practicing time-outs. The more you practice, especially when you're *not* angry, the easier it will be to remember and use a time-out when you really need it. For a practice time-out, say "Practice time-out" while making the "T" sign with your hands. After returning the gesture, each of you should leave for a half-hour and practice the calming exercises or physical activity that you plan to use during a real time-out. When you return, do a mock check-in. Practice as often as you can so that the steps become familiar and easy.

Example: Lily and Joel

Lily and Joel had been married for ten years, and had two children. It had been a stormy relationship, with Lily threatening to leave many times. Their arguments, usually triggered by what both would agree were trivial incidents, tended to escalate rapidly, and usually ended with Lily threatening to leave if Joel didn't change. Sometimes Joel would agree to Lily's request, and each would retreat, emotionally battered and bruised. After which, of course, nothing would change. Other times, Joel would yell something like, "Fine! I'm sick and tired of your threatening. I don't care. Go! Leave!" The he'd turn back to reading his newspaper. Lily would be shocked and hurt, and would sleep on the couch that night. She would keep her distance—physically and emotionally—for the next few days. After which things would return to normal.

This night things began to escalate as rapidly as usual. The kids were asleep, and Joel was lying on the bed reading the newspaper (as usual). Lily was whirling round the house cleaning up the clutter from the kids and the debris from dinner. As she passed the bedroom door and saw Joel stretched out comfortably reading while she wore herself out cleaning, Lily suddenly found herself enraged (again) and unable to tolerate the feelings. "I can't believe you're lying here reading while I'm cleaning up again! Don't you even notice?" she shrieked. Joel looked up from the paper, but didn't wait for Lily to finish her statement. "Cut the crap," he began. "Just because you're running around like a crazy person doesn't mean I have to. Besides, I work forty hours a week to support this family. I think that's enough of a contribution." "Oh God, not that tired old argument again. Forty hours is nothing compared to what I do, and if you don't get that into your thick skull soon. . . ." She trailed off as Joel quickly got up from the bed. He'd suddenly recognized the path they were on and didn't want to go there. As he got up he made the "T" sign, said "Time out," and headed for the door. Lily was about to protest that once again Joel didn't want to address any problems when she remembered their contract. She closed her open mouth and reluctantly made the "T" sign to Joel's retreating back. A few seconds later she heard the front door close softly as Joel started toward the park, a strategy he'd decided upon when they'd first written their Time-out Contract. Lily had decided that her best strategy was to have a bath and focus on relaxing. She ran the bath, poured in some of her favorite bath salts, and put on an old Bill Cosby tape.

An hour later they were both back in the living room. "What do you think?" asked Joel, "Shall we try again?" Lily nodded. "Okay, first, I'm sorry I left so abruptly while you were still talking to me," Joel began. Lily had the grace to blush as she noticed Joel force himself not to say "screaming at me." She hadn't been screaming, but it certainly hadn't been a tone of voice that was conducive to discussion. "I did get upset very quickly," she interjected. "I'm sorry. I just feel so taken for granted sometimes, and I don't like feeling that way. It would make a difference if you helped me out even for a few minutes. Or at least noticed and thanked me for what I was doing."

From here, the discussion proceeded in a totally new way, with Lily agreeing to ask Joel for help when she was feeling overwhelmed or taken for granted, and Joel agreeing to take on the responsibility of cleaning up after dinner, but in his own time.

What If It Fails?

Time Out is a tremendously effective tool when used appropriately. If a time-out fails, it's usually because the guidelines are not being followed accurately. When used manipulatively, a time-out will worsen your relationship. For example, calling a time-out simply because you don't want to discuss something is a manipulative use of the strategy. Time Out doesn't mean that the discussion ends, only that it's postponed until you both are less angry. Calling a time-out after saying something hostile and critical, in an attempt to prevent your partner from responding, is also manipulative. It will leave your partner feeling attacked and more likely compelled to retaliate.

If you call a time-out and your partner follows you from room to room, it's best to leave the environment altogether. Try to plan ahead what each of you will do—and where—when a time-out is called, and enter it in your contract.

There may be times when physically leaving the scene for a time-out isn't feasible. You might be in the car, or at a social or business event. Under those circumstances, you may be able to agree not to talk to each other for the appointed hour. This will enable you to focus on other thoughts or get involved in activities or interactions with others that will distract you from the conflict. When you get home you can then check in with each other and proceed from there.

What Is Negotiation?

When your anger is so intense that talking will inevitably escalate to fighting, there is no place for Negotiation. Time Out is the necessary strategy. When your time-out has been successfully completed and you're both feeling calmer and more in control of your emotions, then it's time to negotiate. Negotiation means talking, and to negotiate effectively, you have to be able to follow specific communication guidelines. You and your partner negotiate all the time, whenever you discuss how to manage your finances, or how to find adequate child care. When you divide the household chores, you're negotiating. Negotiation is a process of working to accommodate two different people with different needs.

Where Does It Come From, and Is It Effective?

Negotiation (for power, land, peace, or commerce) has occurred for centuries, most often accompanied by angry words, rigid ultimatums, desperate stalemates, and ultimately great cost to one or both parties. It wasn't until the 1970s that attention was focused on the most effective way for people to deal with their differences. The Harvard Negotiation Project developed the "one text" mediation procedure that was used in the 1978 Camp David Middle East peace negotiations. Shortly thereafter, their "principled negotiation" method was described in the book *Getting to Yes*, by Roger Fisher and William Ury (1981). This method involved abandoning the hostility of the old ways and focusing instead on mutual interests and possibilities for compromise. Instead of a win-lose paradigm, Negotiation allows both parties to win.

If you're like most couples, your fighting is the result of the mistaken belief that one person's needs (yours) are right and valid and the other person's needs (your partner's) are not. A second assumption many couples make is that in order for one person to win, the other person has to lose. Successful negotiation hinges on two beliefs: First, conflict is normal and inevitable. It's the natural result of two separate people having two different needs and it doesn't necessarily mean that your relationship is on the rocks. Second, both of you have a right to your needs, and those needs are equally valid. Your needs aren't more valid than those of your partner just because you're able to articulate them better; nor are they more important because you can yell louder. Just because you're feeling more pain—or are expressing your pain more dramatically—doesn't make your needs a priority. Equally valid means just that—that both of you are entitled to your needs and to finding a solution that takes all those needs into account. This is an essential belief, and without a solid commitment to it, negotiation will not succeed.

With those beliefs firmly in mind, however, negotiation can proceed toward an outcome that is mutually acceptable for you and your partner, with both of you feeling understood and respected. You probably won't end up with your first choice of outcomes, but most people who negotiate effectively agree that it's a small price to pay for a successful relationship.

When to Use It

When you're aware that your needs aren't being met, and that you and your partner don't seem to be able to find a satisfying outcome, Negotiation can be a useful strategy. Negotiation requires the ability to follow specific communication guidelines. So you need to use it either before a conflict escalates to a point where logic and rationality give way to passionate hostility, or after a time-out has been successfully accomplished. The effectiveness of Negotiation depends on how closely you stick to the principles described below. If you have a genuine desire to compromise, Negotiation will work.

Tools that will facilitate your Negotiation skills include Respectful Anger (chapter 4) and the Four Don'ts (chapter 5).

How to Use It

There are five major stages in any negotiation: preparation, discussion, proposal/counterproposal, disagreement, and agreement.

1. Preparation. When you're angry, your tendency is likely to be to give the preparation stage of negotiation short shrift. In fact, this could be one of the most important stages. It's too easy when you're angry to find yourself arguing for something that really isn't exactly what you want; you're just arguing against what your partner wants in the belief that if your partner wins, you lose. In preparing for a negotiation, it's important to really think about exactly what you want. Think about your ideal, as well as what you could live with, and what's totally unacceptable to you. In order to do this, use the following five steps as a guide: (a) Remind yourself that the goal is for you and your partner to find a mutually agreeable option, and that the more flexible you are, and the fewer preconceived ideas you have, the better. (b) In your mind—or better still, on paper—outline the situation as clearly and unemotionally as possible. (c) Clarify your feelings about the situation. It's important to keep the situation itself separate from your feelings about the situation. (d) Identify what you ideally want in this situation. List your interests, keeping in mind that there are always intangible needs that influence your interests, including the need for respect, for intimacy, for trust, etc. Now list what you imagine your partner's interests are that conflict with your own. Include the intangible needs that you think affect your partner's interests. Try to put yourself in your partner's shoes for a few minutes. Try to imagine what the source of his or her pain is. Underneath the "wants," is he feeling a loss of control that's threatening his feelings of safety and trust? Underneath her demands, is she feeling a lack of respect? Finally, list your shared interests. (e) Clarify your ideal solution to the situation, as well as solutions that you could live with, and the options that are unacceptable.

2. Discussion. The discussion stage is where you and your partner begin to share your information with each other. Take the time to present how you see the situation, what your feelings about it are, and how you see the problem in terms of your conflicting interests and intangible needs. Then listen to how your partner sees and feels about the situation. Only after both of you are clear about these elements is it useful to raise your ideal solutions—as tentative proposals—and listen to those of your partner. Use healthy communication skills. Stay away from blaming, name-calling, labeling, complaining, guilt-tripping, and discounting. Remind yourself that your goal is to come up with a fair, mutually acceptable solution.

3. Proposal/Counterproposal. Once you're both clear what your individual and mutual interests are, it's time to focus on solutions. You raise your ideal proposal, and your partner responds with a counterproposal. You then raise another proposal, a variation of your original proposal that takes some of your partner's interests into account. Your partner then responds with a counterproposal that's closer to meeting your needs. Eventually a compromise solution is developed that's mutually acceptable. There are several strategies that help couples reach compromise. Keep them in mind as you search for agreeable solutions. These strategies, adapted from *Couple Skills* (McKay, Fanning and Paleg 1994), include:

   - I'll cut the pie, you choose your piece first. (I'll divide the list of chores, and you decide which ones you want.)
   - Take turns. (You choose the movie this week; I'll choose it next week.)
   - Do both, have it all. (Let's limit our camping to a week next summer so we have time to attend the reunion.)
   - Trial period. (I'll drop the kids off at soccer practice and you'll pick them up. We can try it for a couple of weeks and see if it works.)
   - My way when I'm doing it, your way when you're doing it. (When I'm with the kids, I'll feed them what I think is

appropriate; when you're with them, you can feed them what you think is appropriate.)

- Tit for tat. (If you do the cooking, I'll do the clean-up.)
- Part of what I want with part of what you want. (You get to bring in a contractor to lay the foundation; I get to do the framing myself.)
- Split the difference. (You want to spend two weeks skiing this winter; I'd rather spend the money on new carpet. Let's split the difference—go skiing for one week and replace the bedroom and living room carpets.)

4. Disagreement. Disagreement is considered a stage by itself because it's inevitable that some negotiations will hit a point where agreement seems impossible. Don't give up. Go back to an earlier stage of the Negotiation process and brainstorm more creative solutions, proposals, or counterproposals. Explore whether there are interests and needs that haven't been fully understood or taken into account. Reexamine your feelings and make sure that you're still committed to finding a mutually agreeable solution.

5. Agreement. With enough perseverance you'll eventually reach a compromise solution that gives you each a maximum of what you want and a minimum of what you don't want. Ensure that both of you are clear and in complete agreement about the chosen solution by repeating it out loud.

Example: Lily and Joel

After the successfully enacted time-out described above, a few weeks passed, during which Lily and Joel had several other time-outs. One night Lily was supervising the after-dinner activities of their two children. "What's for homework tonight?" she asked eight-year-old Ethan. He hesitantly admitted that it was to continue the writing from last night—which he hadn't done. "Did you do any homework last night?" Lily demanded. "Just my reading," Ethan mumbled. Lily was furious. She worked two nights a week, and assumed that Joel supervised Ethan's homework on those nights. In fact, it had been a point of contention in the past and after repeated monologues from Lily, Joel had assured her that she needn't worry about it; he was on top of it. Yet here it was happening again.

Lily waited until both kids were in bed. She sat down at the kitchen table and began writing (Preparation). She described the situation this way: "Ethan gets homework Monday through Thursday. When I'm home, I supervise him. When I work, I can't supervise him. He gets too much homework to do it all on the two nights I'm home with him. Joel doesn't supervise him on the nights I'm working." Describing her feelings about the situation was easy: "I'm frustrated and disappointed. I feel like I'm a single parent shouldering all the responsibility. And I'm worried that not only will Ethan not get his work done and not succeed, but he'll learn from Joel that homework isn't important." Under "interests" Lily wrote for herself: "Not worry about Ethan's homework on nights I work. Not have to be the "bad guy" all the time, pushing him to do the homework. Feel like a team with Joel. Feel like Joel supports the importance of Ethan learning good homework habits." For Joel's interests, Lily wrote: "Relax after a long day at work. Read the paper. Believe Ethan when he says something." She tried to imagine what Joel might be needing underneath his wants. She added "To feel like a good dad. To feel respected and appreciated by me for what he does do." For shared interests, she wrote: "Keep peace between us. Feel close. Have fun with Ethan, not just nag him about homework." From here Lily thought about her ideal solution, which was that on each night that she worked, Joel would ask Ethan to see his homework folder after dinner. Together they would review each assignment, and if any were incomplete, Ethan would do it under Joel's supervision, until both were satisfied that it was complete. She added that she could live with Joel asking to see Ethan's homework, and telling him to go finish it up if it weren't complete. What was unacceptable was Joel not looking at all, but just believing Ethan when he said it was done. She knew Ethan didn't deliberately lie, but he was easily distracted and if he'd done some homework, he often thought he'd done it all.

Thus prepared, Lily went in search of Joel (Discussion). She found him in his usual place, reading the paper in the bedroom. "I can do this," she whispered to herself, as she stood in front of

Joel and took a deep breath. "Joel, I need to talk to you about Ethan's homework," she began. "What about it?" Joel responded. "You agreed to supervise him on the nights I work, and he didn't do it last night," Lily continued. "I asked him if he'd done his homework and he told me he had," Joel defended. "I'm sure that's true," responded Lily, "but that doesn't seem to be working. Look, I've been thinking about this, and I've written some things down. Let me tell you what I've got." Lily went on to explain to Joel how she saw the situation, how she felt about it, and what she understood of their individual and shared interests. "I know you're really tired by the time you get home from work and deal with the kids' dinner and everything, but it would really help if you could look at Ethan's homework with him and go over each assignment to make sure it's all done" (Proposal/Counter-proposal). Joel sighed, "When I ask him about his homework, he tells me either that it's done or that he's too tired to do it. I don't want to fight about it with him." "I know," said Lily. "I don't want to fight about it either. But I notice that when I stay in close touch with him while he does it, go in every few minutes to see how he's doing, he feels okay about it. Like I'm helping him even if I'm not really. I suspect he doesn't like to feel like we're sending him off on his own and ignoring him." "Well, how can I supervise Margot's bath and do her bedtime reading if I'm running in and out of Ethan's room all the time?" Joel protested. "I know," Lily sighed. "It's a lot to do all at the same time. What if you went through the homework before putting Margot in the bath, and then checked on Ethan's progress before reading to her?" she suggested. "Look, I'd be willing to ask Ethan to look at his homework, and remind him to do whatever isn't complete, but then he's old enough to go and do it without my constant presence," Joel stated firmly. "I could have one last look before he goes to bed, but I'm not willing to do more." "I could live with that," Lily acknowledged (Agreement). "So you'll ask to see his homework after dinner, and if it's not complete, send him off to do it while you deal with Margot. Then before it's his bedtime, you'll have one last look?" she repeated just to be sure they were in agreement. "Yeah," Joel said.

What If It Fails?

Sometimes negotiations will fail because one or both partners are too angry to keep focused on the goal of mutual compromise. You may forget the crucial concept that both of you have needs that are equally valid. If either of you engage in blaming, name-calling, guilt-tripping, or discounting, the negotiations will rapidly deteriorate into fighting. You can attempt to prevent this by "calling process." Shift the focus from *what* you're talking about to *how* you're talking about it. "I'm feeling blamed for everything. That's neither fair nor accurate. Let's try to solve the problem without blaming," is an example of calling process when your partner reverts to blaming. "I know you don't like what I've been doing about this, but there's no need to call me names. Let's try to be objective while we look for a better solution." If this doesn't work, and your partner doesn't calm down, you'll have to take a time-out until the necessary communication rules can be appropriately followed.

If your partner is entrenched in his or her position and is unwilling to be flexible, you can adopt a strategy of asking leading questions and waiting for answers. "I think we're pretty stuck on this and need a new plan. Have you got ideas that I don't yet know about?" is an example of this strategy. "I don't think I fully understand why you feel the way you do. Could you please tell me more about it?" is another.

CHAPTER 8

Change the Way You Speak

What Is Language Reform?

Language Reform is a strategy for encouraging nonattacking patterns of communication between angry partners. It's a way to help each of you clean up how you talk so you aren't scarring your relationship with hurtful words and labels.

Language Reform involves three simple steps. First, you each identify the hurtful words that you want your partner to stop using. Second, you each identify reinforcers—up to ten simple things you would enjoy that your partner could do for you. Third, you make a contract: any time one of you uses pejorative words to hurt the other, he or she will compensate with a reinforcer.

Where Does It Come From, and Is It Effective?

Language Reform was developed by the authors in response to research by John Gottman (see chapter 4). Gottman found that chronic criticizing is one of four highly destructive patterns that couples engage in. Clinical studies by Gottman revealed that partners who use highly critical language greatly increase their risk for separation and divorce.

Language Reform achieves two things. First, it has the effect of discouraging pejorative and damaging communication. It makes you far less likely to use words that your partner finds hurtful. Secondly, it makes the relationship more rewarding because you give something to each other as atonement for any hurtful attack.

Our clinical experience with couples reveals that Language Reform reduces the frequency of pejorative labels and profanity. Partners become more aware of their language. They know that using pejoratives will have consequences—they'll have to do something to make up for it.

Language Reform has limitations. It's only as effective as your commitment to use it. That's why we encourage a written contract, preferably signed by a witness who can periodically check in with you and monitor your progress. The more formal and serious the agreement feels, the more likely you are to stick with it.

How to Use It

Step 1, as outlined earlier, is for each partner to identify the pejorative words that he or she wishes to be eliminated. They could be global labels, such as stupid asshole, jerk, selfish, lazy, ice queen, and so on. They could be swear words. They could be epithets like "You don't know jack," or "You're a useless sack of shit." Each of you has the right to list the pejoratives that disturb you most, keeping to an initial limit of five. Whatever you put down on your list essentially becomes forbidden language for your partner.

See the Language Reform Contract later in this chapter for a place to list up to five pejoratives that you want your partner to eliminate.

Step 2 in Language Reform is to identify reinforcers. These should be simple things that would take your partner no more than twenty or thirty minutes to do. Saundra, a working mom, developed the following list for her husband Bill:

Bill could reinforce me by:

- Doing the dishes

- Giving me a neck rub

- Buying flowers

- Getting reservations at a nice restaurant

- Helping with Laura's homework

- Giving me time off in the evening to read and relax

- Taking a walk with me

- Gassing up my car

- Going to the laundromat

- Playing Scrabble with me

Bill's list was a little shorter but included the following.

Saundra could reinforce me by:

- Giving me a head rub

- Meeting me at the door with drink and slippers

- Giving me time off at night to relax

- Putting the kids to bed for me

- Walking the dog

- Making Swiss steak or chicken à l'orange for dinner

- Making a rhubarb pie

- Making dumplings

Bill obviously had gastronomic interests that Saundra didn't share. But each of them created a list of reinforcers that uniquely satisfied them. You may have noticed that none of the items include exchanging sexual favors or money. There's a good reason for that. Sex and money are areas that are simply too charged and dangerous to inject into a program of atonement.

Make a list like the one shown on the next page, in a notebook or on a single sheet of paper. You should each list up to ten small reinforcers that can be used as compensation if your partner uses any of the hurtful words you've agreed to eliminate.

Reinforcers

Partner: _____

  1.

  2.

  3.

  4.

  5.

  6.

  7.

  8.

  9.

10.

Partner: _____

  1.

  2.

  3.

  4.

  5.

  6.

  7.

  8.

  9.

10.

The third and last step in Language Reform is to make a written contract. On the next page, you'll find an example contract that we urge you to use. If, for any reason, this contract doesn't work for you, modify it so it feels more appropriate.

Notice that the contract stipulates that multiple uses of a single pejorative earn a single reinforcer. That's so someone won't end up owing twenty reinforcers because they said "stupid" twenty times during a fight. Each *different* pejorative, however, does earn a separate reinforcer. We encourage you to have a witness sign the contract so it has a certain formality. It's also helpful if the witness agrees to check in with you at regular intervals about your Language Reform contract and how well your program is going. It doesn't matter whether the witness is a friend or family member. What's important is that they take seriously their role and actually follow through with the check-ins.

Example: Robert and Selena

A couple that we worked with, Robert and Selena, had a fairly typical experience with Language Reform. After identifying pejoratives and reinforcers, they signed the standard contract (see below). Selena's best friend signed as a witness.

During the first week, they used one of the listed pejoratives four different times between them, and they followed with reinforcers within twenty-four hours. They reported that the reinforcers were fun and actually gave the relationship a boost. During the second week, the use of pejoratives was cut in half. However, Selena kept forgetting to give Robert his reinforcer. Only after her best friend called to check in did she manage to follow through with it.

The third week there were no pejoratives. The fourth week had one. The fifth, sixth, and seventh weeks had no reports of pejoratives. There was a relapse in week eight, but that was the last reported pejorative exchanged for this couple.

Language Reform Contract

We agree to no longer use the pejoratives listed here.

_____ will no longer say:

1. _____

2. _____

3. _____

4. _____

5. _____

_____ will no longer say:

1. _____

2. _____

3. _____

4. _____

5. _____

If either of us uses a listed pejorative, he or she will compensate the other with one of his or her reinforcers. Whoever used the pejorative gets to choose the reinforcer. Compensation will occur within twenty-four hours. Multiple use of a single pejorative earns a single reinforcer. Each *different* pejorative earns a separate reinforcer.

Date: _____

Partner: _____
                              (signature)

Partner: _____
                              (signature)

Witness: _____
                              (signature)

What If It Fails?

Language Reform works. If you stick with it, we guarantee there will be a lot less pain in your relationship. But what if your partner doesn't want to participate in the exercise? You can still reform your own language. Even with just one party skipping the pejoratives, you'll find that arguments don't escalate as much.

CHAPTER 9

Create an Anger Coping Plan

What Is an Anger Coping Plan?

Your angry reactions are a well-worn habit. They may feel almost as reflexive as that little kick you give when the doctor hits your knee with the rubber mallet. But what's habitual doesn't have to be inevitable. The way to change automatic, habitual behavior is to plan ahead. The trick is to develop new coping strategies while you're calm and relaxed and far away from all provocations.

Anger Coping Plans have four components:

1. a quick relaxation exercise

2. an assertive request

3. a de-escalation strategy

4. prevention problem solving

Each component of your plan provides an effective alternative response to anger. Used together, they greatly diminish your chance of repeating old, damaging patterns.

Where Does It Come From, and Is It Effective?

The Anger Coping Plan used here was adapted from one developed by Jerry Deffenbacher and Matthew McKay (2000). It is a component of the most extensively researched and widely used anger management protocol currently available.

Planning works. Research shows that the more carefully you plan a new behavioral response, the more likely you are to remember that new response during an emotionally charged situation. Behavioral planning is also associated with better outcomes. People report feeling more satisfied with the way they handle problem situations when they have planned an effective response and developed specific strategies to handle predictable difficulties.

How to Use It

Right now you should identify a recurring conflict—an issue or situation that keeps triggering anger for you and your partner. It should be something that happens relatively often, preferably on occasions where you can see it coming. For example, if you often have conflict about the bills, you might devise a coping plan for the next time you sit down to pay them. Or if you tend to have upsets when you're tired and stressed right after work, you'd do well to have a coping plan to help you better manage when you get home. Using the criteria that the anger situation should be relatively frequent and predictable, choose one you want to work on.

In a moment, you're going to do something that will be an important step in changing how this traditional conflict plays out. You're going to map out the fight sequence using the Escalation Ramp exercise on page 109. The diagonal line going from "start" to "blowup" represents the escalating sequence of events as the fight unfolds. In your notebook, just fill in what each of you said or did on the horizontal lines, beginning with the very first irritant and ending where the fight reaches its apex. For an example of a completed Escalation Ramp, see Sandy's Escalation Ramp on page 117.

Try to get as much detail and as many steps as possible documented on the ramp.

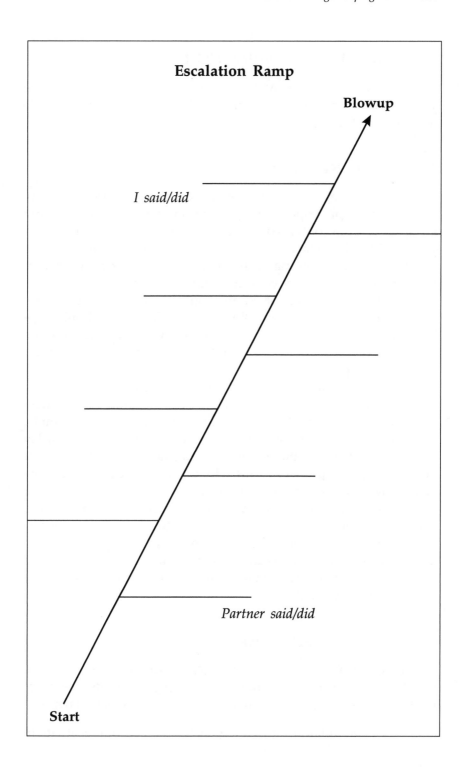

Your Anger Coping Plan

Take a look at the Anger Coping Plan Worksheet on page 115. As you formulate your plan, you'll be copying this template into your notebook.

Step 1: Relaxation

To better cope with any provocation, you need to relax away tension *before* you respond. The best technique for relaxing during an upset is Cue-Controlled Breathing (see chapter 2). Right now, you need to plan when, exactly, during the anger event you'll use Cue-Controlled Breathing. Then, you should identify a *reminder* that will help you keep your commitment to relax.

Look at the Escalation Ramp you've just completed. Where in that sequence can you breathe and relax? Ideally, it should happen (1) before the tension gets too high, and (2) at a stage in the escalation process where you have the time and space to focus on your breathing.

Under Relaxation Strategy on your Anger Coping Plan Worksheet, write the exact point on the escalation ramp where you plan to utilize Cue-Controlled Breathing. For example, Amelio, who often fought with his wife during the Saturday house cleanup, chose the moment when Martha said, "We'd best get at it." With those words, his wife inevitably began the discussion of who did what on Saturday morning.

Under Relaxation Strategy, you also need to note how you'll *remind* yourself to do Cue-Controlled Breathing. It could be wearing a certain piece of jewelry, an attention-getting garment, even an agreement that your partner will remind you to relax. Amelio decided to wear his garish Hawaiian shirt on Saturday as a cue to use his relaxation skills.

Step 2: Assertive Request

Planning ahead to prevent angry conflict requires that you script a clear, assertive statement regarding your needs (see chapter 4 on I Messages). An assertive request has three components:

- a clear, nonattacking statement of the facts of the situation

- an "I" statement describing your feelings in the situation

- a specific request for something you want changed

Under Assertive Request on your Anger Coping Plan, write a brief script covering the above three components. Amelio's script looked like this:

- "Martha, you usually assign the tasks each of us will handle during Saturday cleanup. Later, I tend to avoid or do a half-hearted job on things I've been assigned."

- "I often feel resentful about how things are divided up, but don't say anything initially."

- "I'd like us to make a list of the chores and take turns choosing from the list—like team captains choosing their players. That way we'd each have a shot at choosing some of the tasks we like best, and nobody'd feel stuck with the real bummer chores."

Step 3: De-Escalation

There are three options to choose from for de-escalating:

1. acknowledging your partner's feelings and needs

2. finding an "intervention point" to stop the Escalation Ramp

3. taking a time-out

To effectively acknowledge your partner's feelings and needs, you'll need to fill out a Couples Research Form (see chapter 3 on Empathy Training) regarding this conflict. Use the Research Form to get enough information to identify your partner's concerns. For example, when Amelio interviewed Martha, he learned something very important about her feelings regarding the house. Martha told him: "When the house is dirty or messy, I feel depressed. It visually assaults me. Everywhere I look, something makes me feel bad . . . I basically assign you chores because I'm afraid they'll never get done if I don't take charge and push you. And even with all my pushing and nagging, they often don't get done. I end up feeling crappy all week when I look around the house."

Amelio distilled what he learned from this interview into a simple statement acknowledging how Martha felt. Under De-escalation on his Anger Coping Plan, Amelio wrote the following: "Martha, I realize a messy or dirty house affects you and makes you feel bad all week. And you feel like you have to take charge of the chores because I don't take initiative myself."

Notice how this statement validates Martha's experience and makes it clear that Amelio understands her feelings and concerns. You can imagine how powerful this kind of acknowledgment is in calming troubled waters.

The second option for de-escalating is finding an intervention point on the Escalation Ramp. Review the Ramp you drew earlier in the chapter. Look for an intervention point early in the process, before the anger runs too high. What would you say or do differently at this point to change the course of the argument?

In some conflicts, it might be replacing a key blaming statement with a clear, assertive request, or changing specific problem behavior. It might be apologizing briefly for your partner's distress. It could be taking a deep breath and saying, "Let's relax and cool down. We can figure this out." It might be suggesting a proposed solution instead of denigrating a partner's needs. For Amelio, the intervention point was when he started putting Martha down for her "Mr. Clean fetish." There always seemed to be a point during the chores (usually when Martha complained that he wasn't doing them) that Amelio criticized his wife's need for order and cleanliness. Instead he decided to say, "We have different needs here, and it makes it hard for both of us."

A second intervention point for Amelio was how he typically put off getting to the chores. He decided to start immediately after breakfast and set a two-hour deadline for finishing. That was a lot better than wasting the day, procrastinating, and fighting with Martha.

The third option for de-escalating is to take a time-out (see chapter 7 for details of the Time-Out Contract). If things tend to get nasty fast, with a rapid-fire exchange of blame or criticism, a time-out may be the best way to prevent further emotional scarring. To use Time Out effectively, follow these guidelines:

1. agree with your partner in advance that the time-out signal will stop this conflict in its tracks

2. establish a one-hour period for the time-out

3. make an appointment for a time in the future when you'll negotiate a compromise solution

Amelio planned to use Time Out if he and Martha started raising their voices. At the first sign that the volume was going up, he would leave the house for an hour. When he came back, he'd try to offer an alternative solution to the conflict. Failing that, he'd set a time later that day to negotiate with Martha about the chores.

Step 4: Prevention Problem Solving

Here the effort is to plan a solution that changes the situation entirely. You no longer need to fight, because the conflict or irritant is resolved. The key is to propose something that takes care of both of you. One-sided solutions don't work. (See chapter 7 on Negotiation.)

Amelio had several ideas for prevention problem solving that he included in his Anger Coping Plan:

- hiring a four-hour-per-week house cleaner

- trading off the chore he hated most (tub and toilet)

- setting a deadline to finish and asking Martha not to nag him unless the deadline passed

- taking turns choosing from a list of chores

He decided to discuss these with Martha over dinner during the week when they were relaxed and feeling good with each other.

Notice that the exclusive focus of the Anger Coping Plan is *your behavior*. That's because your behavior is all you can control; it's all you're capable of changing. Focusing on getting your partner to change is an exercise in futility, and only serves to keep the fighting going. Because the Anger Coping Plan is unilateral, it assumes nothing about your partner's responses. You can, however, be sure of one thing: if you change your behavior, your partner's behavior will change too.

On the next page is an Anger Coping Plan Worksheet. This page probably isn't big enough for all the writing you'll need to do, but it shows you the format to use on your own 8 ½-by-11 sheet. Fill out a worksheet whenever you want to plan ahead to change the conflict situations you encounter frequently.

Visualization to Rehearse Your Coping Plan

Visualization is a simple, easy way to practice your new coping strategies. To get started, go back to the Escalation Ramp you filled out and replace some of your provocative behavior with items from the Coping Plan. Just cross out what you said or did, and write above it what you plan to say or do instead. For example, write in where you plan to do some Cue-Controlled Breathing, where you'll make your assertive requests, where you'll acknowledge your partner, where your main intervention point will be, etc.

Assume, on your partner's side, that he or she responds pretty much as usual, but have it end with two different scenarios:

1. Your partner eventually comes around and begins a calm discussion with you regarding the issues and possible solutions.

2. Your partner keeps escalating and you call a time-out.

Now sit back in a chair, close your eyes, and imagine the escalation sequence—but with your new coping behavior plugged in for your old habitual responses. When you reach the point in the unfolding scene where you use Cue-Controlled Breathing, actually do it. When you reach the point where you make an assertive request, imagine each detail of the three-part statement (facts, feelings, request). When you reach your intervention point on the Escalation Ramp, visualize what exactly you'll say or do to implement this new strategy.

On the other side, imagine your partner continuing for a time to be difficult. Then end the visualization with either a

Anger Coping Plan Worksheet

Anger Situation (chosen for frequency and predictability):

Escalation Ramp (use separate sheet):

Plan:

1. Relaxation Strategy
   - Where on escalation ramp?

   - Reminder?

2. Assertive Request
   - Statement of the facts:

   - I Message describing your feelings:

   - Specific request:

3. De-escalation
   - Acknowledging partner's feelings and needs:

   - Intervention point—where? What will you do or say differently?

   - Time Out—when and how:

4. Prevention Problem Solving (list alternative solutions):

   a.

   b.

   c.

time-out or a shift to a calm discussion. Be sure to practice the visualization both ways. And speaking of practice, the more you rehearse your coping plan through visualization, the more likely you are to succeed with it.

Example: Sandy and Bill

Sandy disliked traveling with her partner, Bill. Bill was both very cheap and very particular about motel accommodations. They often ended up going to three or four places before he found one to his liking. Sometimes he'd actually check in, find some fault in the room, and have Sandy repack so they could begin the search again. It wasn't uncommon for Bill to end up in the first place he'd looked at, after checking out multiple motels in between.

A fight almost invariably happened after Bill rejected the second or third motel. Here's how Sandy filled out the escalation ramp.

Sandy's Escalation Ramp

Blowup

Humiliating public fight at the front desk.

I get my bags out of the trunk and try to check into a separate room.

He pulls up to another motel, gets out, slams the door, and heads for the front desk.

I said/did

"Go F yourself," I'm screaming.

He gets angry and says he's going to kick me out of the car if I don't shut up.

I get attacking—call him stupid, cheap, compulsive, etc.

He pouts and gives the silent treatment.

"For Christ's sake, make up your mind or I'm going home."

He says the second or third motel is too dirty, too expensive, or doesn't have a good view, etc.

Partner said/did

Start

Sandy then made a coping plan to alter the fight sequence and substitute new strategies for some of her old, angry behavior.

Sandy's Anger Coping Plan

Anger Situation: Bill looking for some cheap but beautiful motel.

Plan:

1. Relaxation Strategy
   - Where on escalation ramp? When Bill rejects second motel.
   - Reminder? Wear Grandma's spoon ring and my paisley dress.

2. Assertive Request
   - Facts: "Bill, we're headed for our third motel, something we frequently do when traveling."
   - Feelings: "I'm tired and stressed. I need to relax and put my feet up. I feel myself losing patience."
   - Request: "Please, either pick one of the two motels we've already been to, or the next motel we check—no matter what it costs or looks like—has to be the one. Your choice."

3. De-Escalate
   - Acknowledge: "I know it makes you anxious and kind of spoils the trip for you if we spend more than seventy-five dollars a night. And it's depressing to be on vacation and stay in an ugly place that doesn't look out on anything. I totally understand that."
   - Intervention Point: Where I get attacking. I'll say, "Bill, I'm a basket case. The next motel has to be it. I'm checking in there, and I hope you'll join me."
   - Time-Out: Where he says he's going to kick me out of the car and before I start screaming. We don't talk until after we've checked into a motel—which will be the next place because I'll check in by myself, if need be.

---

4. Prevention Problem Solving
- I'll call ahead and make reservations at the best place I can find for under seventy-five dollars. If he doesn't like it, we'll check in anyway. Then he can go off and search by himself. If he finds a place he prefers, we'll move over there.

Finally, Sandy reworked her Escalation Ramp using items from the coping plan. Then she visualized the fight sequence with her new coping responses. She imagined Bill reacting in his usual way at the beginning of the fight, but eventually coming around to a rational discussion. She also imagined a scenario where he continued to be angry, and she had to call a time-out. Sandy made four or five passes through the visualization before she and Bill took their next weekend trip. It helped her keep control when he rejected the second motel because "the room had no coffee maker." She immediately did Cue-Controlled Breathing, and made her assertive request. Bill grumped, but reluctantly checked into the third motel. Six weeks later, when they took another weekend jaunt, Sandy got advance reservations, checked in, and watched an entire movie while Bill drove all over town looking in vain for better accommodations. When he returned, she was relaxed, and had already selected a moderately priced Chinese restaurant for their dinner.

What If It Fails?

If you stick with your Anger Coping Plan, you will definitely see results. This multifaceted approach really works.

CHAPTER 10

Give Your Partner Pleasure

What Is Pleasure Exchange?

Pleasure exchange rebuilds trust and goodwill in relationships scarred by anger. It involves an exchange between partners of small, easily-accomplished gifts of time or energy. These gifts can range from a kiss or a compliment to cooking a special dinner or fixing the broken screen door.

When you're really angry at your partner it's hard to even imagine doing something loving. You'd rather ignore his or her very existence than spontaneously offer a cup of tea, give a foot massage, or bring flowers. Instead of exchanging fond smiles it seems easier to exchange hostilities.

It's time now to break that pattern. Acting "as if" you were interested in a warm, loving relationship can enhance warm, loving feelings. The pleasure exchange will not only thaw out your partner, it will help you feel closer as well.

Where Does It Come From, and Is It Effective?

R. B. Stuart introduced a concept called "reciprocal reinforcement" to couples therapy in 1969. By directing each person to select three pleasing behaviors that their partner could perform easily, Stuart helped couples increase the number of positive experiences in their relationships. His intervention was based on his observation that distressed couples often have particularly low rates of positive interactions and his belief that "positive actions are likely to induce positive reactions, first in the attitudes of others, and then in their behaviors" (1980, 194). "Caring days" were assigned where each person was asked to focus on performing an especially high number of "caring" behaviors for his or her partner.

The "fun deck" is a tool developed by Markman and Floyd (1980) to enhance the positive elements of an otherwise troubled relationship. A couple brainstorms a list of fun activities, then each partner selects from that list their three favorite activities. After exchanging their "favorites" lists, each person commits to ensuring that at least one thing from their partner's list happens in the following week.

If your relationship is plagued by anger and hostility and it's hard to even remember the pleasurable interactions, you can remedy the situation by either decreasing the negative interactions or increasing the positive, pleasurable ones. In the long term, you need to eliminate the critical, hostile interactions to build a better relationship. However, in the short term you can provide the foundation and motivation for doing the long-term work by increasing the positive feelings between you and your partner. Pleasure exchange gives you a structured way to pursue increased pleasure in your relationship.

In this way, pleasure exchange is an effective tool in the fight against hostility. It's far easier to do positive things than to stop doing negative things. That's especially true when the positive things are all familiar and easily accomplished (a kiss, a compliment, cooking a favorite dessert, etc.). Think about it this way: you have an immediate reaction when your partner deliberately does something that she or he knows pisses you off. Well, there's an equally immediate—and opposite—reaction when your partner deliberately does something that he or she knows you find pleasurable. Knowing that you have the power to elicit the same reaction in your partner can build your confidence. Furthermore, by acting "as if" you feel better about your partner and want to behave in more caring ways, you will eventually begin to feel better about your partner and genuinely want to be more caring and loving.

When to Use It?

Pleasure exchange can be used at any time. When your relationship is feeling relatively calm, it will simply make a good thing better. When your relationship is feeling more rocky, pleasure exchange can provide a focus for regenerating positive feelings. When you're in the middle of a fight, however, Time Out should first be used to prevent unnecessary escalation. Once you're both calm, pleasure exchange can be useful again. When conflicts need to be addressed using Negotiation and I Messages, pleasure exchange makes a useful supplementary strategy.

How to Use It?

There are five steps in the effective use of pleasure exchange, including the development and use of the "fun deck." Those steps are as follows:

1. List pleasing behaviors and rank them 1, 2, or 3.

2. Exchange lists.

3. Choose three items from your partner's list to do each day.

4. Develop a "fun deck."

5. Commit to each making one activity happen.

Step 1 in effective pleasure exchange is to make your respective lists of pleasing behaviors. Carry around a pen and paper for a week and write down all the things your partner does that please you or make you feel cared for. At this point you might feel like there aren't that many. Nevertheless, try to notice everything, from household management decisions to communication patterns, from issues of personal appearance and grooming, to small considerate gestures. Add to that list things that you'd like your partner to do, or things that he or she might have once done but doesn't anymore. Look for small things that are easy to accomplish.

It's important that you focus on specific behaviors rather than attitudes or feelings. It's okay to ask your partner to accompany you on your evening walks in the park. It doesn't make sense to ask him to *want* to exercise more. Nor is it useful to ask for vague, general behaviors. "Give me a hug and kiss before going to bed" is more specific—and therefore more easily accomplished—than "be more affectionate." "Call me when you're going to be late" is more specific—and less critical—than "be more responsible." It's also essential that your list include only those behaviors that don't involve huge expense or effort. Eliminate such items as "Take me on a cruise" or "Lose forty pounds." Also eliminate items that pertain to matters of major conflict in your relationship.

When you have at least a dozen items on your lists, rank the items 1, 2, or 3, where 1 is nice, 2 is better, and 3 is great. Whereas a kiss before leaving in the morning may be nice and rank a 1, a foot massage while watching a video may be great and rank a 3. Similarly, your partner offering to make you a cup of tea after dinner may rank a 1, calling to say she's going to be late may rank a 2, and stopping on the way home to pick up some groceries may be a 3.

When ranking is complete, step 2 is to exchange lists with your partner. Review your partner's list carefully, noticing not only the items that are on the list, but also those that are not. There are probably several things that you do to show your desire to please your partner that aren't on his or her list. Check out with your partner whether he or she would like to include those things on his or her list, but don't be surprised—or offended—if the answer is No. You are separate, independent people with your own likes and dislikes, your own values and histories. What gives you pleasure and makes you feel cared for doesn't necessarily give your partner pleasure. And what you've interpreted in the past as appreciation from your partner in response to some behavior of yours may in fact have been appreciation of the gesture rather than pleasure in the behavior itself.

When you review your partner's list, make sure that there's nothing on the list that you're unwilling to do. If there is, tell your partner and have him or her cross it off the list. If you have an aversion to baths, you're unlikely to agree to soak in a hot bath with your partner. If you can't stomach the idea of wearing sexy lingerie, you're unlikely to indulge his fantasies in that way. When both lists have been amended as necessary, make several copies of each and place them in easy-to-see places around the house.

For step 3, choose three things from your partner's list to do each day, ensuring that at least one of the items is ranked 3. Don't pick the same three things each day, and don't inform your partner what your choices are from day to day. At the end of the week, review your progress with your partner. If the items on the lists—or their ranks—need some revision, do it now. Keep in mind that the more things you do from your partner's list of pleasers, the faster you'll build positive feelings in the relationship, and the more motivation you both will have for eliminating the negative interactions. Remember to let your partner know that the pleasers did in fact please you.

As impossible as it may sound initially, it's essential that you complete your three caring activities gracefully and openheartedly, with a true desire to make your partner feel cared for and valued. Just going through the motions will be experienced by your partner as, at best, a reluctant effort to please him or her and, at worst, a sign of contempt and disrespect.

Once you've practiced the daily pleasure exchange, it's time to move to step 4 and develop the "fun deck." A fun deck is a list of activities that the two of you enjoy (or used to enjoy—or even think you *might* enjoy) doing together. The activities could include hiking, sailing, horseback riding, going to a movie or the theatre, sitting in a hot tub, going to a jazz club, dancing, exploring a new part of the area, eating out, flying a kite, rock climbing, walking on the beach, playing tennis, bowling, or any other activities.

Brainstorm your list of fun activities together. Don't hold back on your suggestions. The more activities on your list, the greater the chances that you'll end up with some really fun possibilities. Think about all the things you used to enjoy doing together, as well as the things you've always wanted to try. Remember not to judge or criticize your partner's suggestions; you'll have time to evaluate the options later. And stay away from activities that have been the source of stress or conflict. If you've always gotten competitive when you play racquetball together, leave that off your list.

Once you've pooled all your ideas, go through the list together and eliminate any activities that either of you have strong negative feelings about. This process of elimination ensures that the activities that remain on the list at the end of the procedure are ones that both of you think would be fun. If you have fewer than six activities left on your revised list, you'll need to either brainstorm more ideas, or go back over the originally rejected activities and rethink your decision to eliminate them.

The next step is for each of you to pick your three favorite activities and write them down. Exchange lists with your partner. Each of you should select at least one of your partner's activities and make sure it happens during the following week.

Example: Sandy and Todd

The conflict between Sandy and Todd had been so painful for so long that, by unspoken agreement, they led virtually parallel lives. They alternated daily parenting responsibilities and they only occasionally organized weekend activities together. Their interactions were limited to topics of household management and their three children, and were often conducted in tight, angry, clipped voices, though neither could have described what they were angry about most of the time. Both felt lonely and disappointed in their relationship and blamed the other for not putting any effort into making it work. However, for the kids' sake they were determined not to divorce, so leading somewhat separate lives seemed better than leading lives of constant conflict.

When they first learned about pleasure exchange, both Sandy and Todd were skeptical. They felt burned out and resentful. They were uncertain about whether they were willing to do more work without the other partner doing it first. But after due consideration they decided that they really had nothing to lose and would therefore give it a try.

The first step was for each of them to make a list of the behaviors their partner did or could do that would please them, and then to rank them 1 (nice), 2 (better), or 3 (great). For a week Sandy and Todd edged around each other with their pens and paper, adding things to their respective lists. The usual tension between them had dissipated a little, and both felt a barely perceptible sense of optimism. At the end of the week their lists were as follows:

Sandy's Pleasure List

Say hello to me when I arrive home after you—2

Give me a kiss when I arrive home or leave—3

Kiss me (at any other time!)—3

Give me a hug—2

Offer me a cup of tea after dinner—1

Hang around with me while I'm taking care of the kids—2

Initiate a conversation—3

Ask me how my day was—3

Bring me flowers—2

Bring me a card or small gift—1

Call me from the office just to say hello—2

Give me a back rub or foot massage—3

Run me a bath—1

Compliment me on my appearance—2

Thank me after I cook dinner, and tell me the food was good—1

Say something nice about me (in front of me) to others—3

Hold my hand or cuddle with me when we watch a video—3

Hold my hand when we go out somewhere—2

Clean up after the kids—2

Todd's Pleasure List

Offer to do my laundry—2

Tell me you love me—3

Dress up for me—3

Make my favorite dinner—1

Hold my hand in the movies—1

Ask my opinion about things—3

Call me at work to say hello—1

Initiate sex—3

Tell me what you like about me—3

Make coffee for me in the morning—2

Watch the news with me at night—2

Greet me with a kiss when I come home after you—2

Wear my favorite perfume—1

Ask me how my day was—3

Tell me about your day—3

With some trepidation, Todd and Sandy exchanged their lists. They read each other's lists, noticing with some surprise that none of the items looked especially difficult, certainly nothing that they would be unwilling to do—sooner or later. They hadn't made love in a long time, so initiating lovemaking felt a little premature to Sandy, but not impossible—not if Todd were to actually do some of the things on her list.

Over the next week, Todd and Sandy picked three things from each other's list to do each day, making sure that at least one of the three things was rated a 3. The first day Todd gave Sandy a kiss when he left for work, and another one when he got home. He told her that the dinner she cooked was good, and offered to make her a cup of tea afterward. Sandy made Todd a cup of coffee in the morning before he left for work, asked him how his day was during dinner, and sat and watched the news with him after the kids were in bed. Things felt a little stilted, but it was the first affectionate contact they'd had in a long time—and it felt good.

At the end of the week both were aware of a definite warming of the habitual chill between them. They had been able to discuss how their respective days had been without a fight, and had even talked briefly about a note they had received from their daughter's teacher. They reviewed their lists and neither felt the need to change anything, so they decided to simply continue. After another two weeks both felt ready to develop a fun deck.

At the assigned time, Sandy brought a pen and a piece of paper to the kitchen table and they both sat down—next to each other. They knew what the task was—to come up with a list of activities that would be fun to do together, just the two of them. First they brainstormed, with Sandy writing down all the ideas they tossed out. Their original list looked like this:

Sandy and Todd's Pleasure List

1. Go to a movie

2. Hike in the mountains

3. Go out dancing

4. Learn to skydive

5. Go to a fancy restaurant for dinner

6. Go roller skating

7. Walk on the beach

8. Go to a hot tub

9. Go to a jazz club

10. Learn to parasail

11. Go rock climbing

12. Go to the races

13. Go fishing

14. Go to estate auctions

When they went through the list to eliminate the items either of them didn't want, only #4 (learn to skydive) and #12 (go to the races) were eliminated. Todd decided that his life was risky enough without jumping out of airplanes. Sandy realized that it made sense to avoid activities that had been the focus of past conflict. Many past fights had arisen from trips to the races where she thought Todd bet a little too freely and lost a little too much money.

From the remaining twelve activities, Sandy and Todd each selected their top three favorites. Both of them knew that their ability to sit and face each other for any length of time without arguing was still pretty rudimentary. So Sandy chose: go out dancing, go rock climbing, walk on the beach. Todd chose: go roller skating, go to a jazz club, hike in the mountains.

The last step in the process of the fun deck was for Sandy and Todd to choose one activity from each other's top three list and commit to organizing that activity for the following week. Since the weather was cooperating, Todd chose to plan a walk on the beach. Finding a babysitter at short notice was always an issue, so to ensure the success of his plan, Todd asked Sandy to keep Friday lunchtime free. Fridays were light days for both of them, as well as "dress down" days, and an occasional long lunch hour wasn't frowned on. At noon Todd collected Sandy from her office, having stopped at a deli on the way to buy a picnic lunch, and headed to the coast. For an hour they meandered together along the beach, skipping stones and gathering shells. Even without much verbal interaction, it felt like a breakthrough.

Sandy, meanwhile, chose going to a jazz club as her activity to arrange. She arranged for her mother to sit with the kids, and bought tickets for Saturday night at a local club. On the heels of their beach walk, it didn't matter that the group playing wasn't great. They enjoyed being out, being together, and not talking about or fighting about their problems.

What If It Fails?

It's unlikely that correctly using the strategy of pleasure exchange will fail to result in an increase in positive feelings between you and your partner in as little as a week. If this isn't happening, you need to ask yourself if you're really committed to improving your relationship. You have to be willing to do the activity regardless of what you perceive your partner doing. If you wait for your partner to do his or her caring behaviors first, no change will occur. Similarly, if you're just going through the motions, you might as well not do anything at all.

If your attitude is not the problem, review the lists of caring behaviors that you wrote and exchanged. Ensure that the items on the lists are specific, easy to accomplish behaviors. Eliminate items that are vague, involve huge effort or expense, require a change in attitude, or reflect a negative request, i.e. "Be *less*. . . ."

When you set about accomplishing at least three items daily from your partner's list, make sure you don't pick the same three things each day. Don't undermine the activity by informing your partner of your behavior while in progress, and don't test your partner to see if he or she is noticing. Most importantly, try not to keep track of who's done how many caring behaviors and when.

Afterword

The fundamental problem each couple must face is how to deal with conflict. Inevitably, you have different needs and values regarding space, intimacy, recreation, lifestyle, aesthetics, order, sharing of tasks, and a host of other issues. When the honeymoon is over, you begin to recognize just how big the gap may be in some of these key areas.

Most people feel a little scared and discouraged at this point. They wonder if these emerging conflicts are the tip of the iceberg; whether sooner or later the ship will go down. And they tend to cope using strategies learned in their families of origin. That's where the problem starts. Lots of people grow up in families that use *aversive strategies* to solve problems, and these strategies become a model for handling conflicts in a new relationship. If you watched your parents discounting, blaming, threatening, belittling, guilt-tripping, or pouting to force a partner to change, you may find yourself slipping into similar patterns when you and your spouse don't see eye-to-eye.

Aversive strategies usually have an angry base—the under-lying message to the other person is "you're bad." And the strategies are often successful in the short run. Your partner may feel hurt and try extra hard to please you. But that gets old, and sooner or later they withdraw or get angry themselves. They stop caring what you want, or how you feel. They build an emotional fortress that your anger can't penetrate. Now conflict really gets ugly. When you confront a situation where you have different needs, things escalate quickly. Old frustrations and scars fuel a rapid lashing back and forth. You pound away with words. But no one listens.

Perhaps the most painful outcome of using aversive strategies is the development of a pursuer-distancer pattern. One of you flails away with anger, while the other withdraws into deeper and deeper emotional isolation. The more the pursuer tries to blame, belittle, or threaten a partner into changing, the more the distancer hardens and shuts down. The emergence of the pursuer-distancer pattern is highly predictive of divorce.

All this can change, starting right now. This book is giving you the tools to literally start over. Now, when you encounter conflicting needs, you can negotiate, use the Couple's Research Form, or try Role Reversal. If you don't feel you're being heard, you can use assertive I Messages. The old, aversive strategies are no longer useful because the new communication tools work better. Not only can you get more of what you need, but you can do so without scarring your relationship.

For the first time now, a little upset doesn't have to end in thermonuclear rage. You have ways to stop things from blowing up: Time Out, De-Escalation, Cue-Controlled Relaxation, and Language Reform. You should also have a Coping Plan to help you navigate through turbulent "white water" conflicts and traditional anger triggers.

You no longer have to retreat, licking your wounds, seething with unexpressed rage. Now you can use strategies such as Stop and Breathe and the Eye Movement Technique. Perhaps most important, the old pursuer-distancer pattern can begin to reverse. Instead of pulling up the drawbridge, you can use the Pleasure Exchange and Empathy Building exercises to get closer again. Those thick walls, so long needed for protection, can be left behind. You can be as open and easy with each other as you were, long ago, before all the hurts started.

Krishnamurti once said that only when you really know something, can it change. You know how painful it is to live in the grip of anger. You know that the attacking and blaming have solved none of the problems between you. For all the shouting, you are never heard. For all the struggle, you remain helpless. This is the time when change is truly possible. This is the moment to let go of the past and use your new tools to build a closer, happier life together.

References

Clements, M. L., A. D. Cordova, H. J. Markman, and J-P. Laurenceau. 1997. The erosion of marital satisfaction over time and how to prevent it. In *Satisfaction in Close Relationships*, edited by R. J. Sternberg and M. Hojjat. New York: Guilford Press.

Davis, M., E. R. Eshelman, and M. McKay. 2000. *The Relaxation & Stress Reduction Workbook*. Oakland, Calif.: New Harbinger Publications.

Deffenbacher, J. L., and M. McKay. 2000. *Overcoming Situational and General Anger (Therapist Protocol)*. Oakland, Calif.: New Harbinger Publications.

Deschner, J. P. 1984. *The Hitting Habit*. New York: The Free Press.

Fisher, R., and W. Ury. 1981. *Getting to Yes: Negotiating Agreements Without Giving In*. Boston: Houghton Mifflin.

Gottman, J. 1997. A Scientifically-Based Marital Therapy: A Workshop for Clinicians. Clinical Manual for Marital Therapy. Seattle: The Seattle Marital and Family Institute, Inc.

Gottman, J. 1994. *Why Marriages Succeed or Fail*. New York: Simon & Schuster.

Markman, H. J., and F. Floyd. 1980. Possibilities for the prevention of marital discord: A behavioral perspective. *American Journal of Family Therapy* 8, 29-48.

Markman, H. J., and K. Hahlweg. 1993. The prediction and prevention of marital distress: An international perspective. *Clinical Psychology Review* 13, 29-43.

McKay, M., and P. D. Rogers. 2000. *The Anger Control Workbook.* Oakland, Calif.: New Harbinger Publications.

McKay, M., M. Davis, and P. Fanning. 1983. *Messages.* Oakland, Calif.: New Harbinger Publications.

McKay, M., P. Fanning, K. Paleg. 1994. *Couple Skills.* Oaklnad, Calif.: New Harbinger Publications.

Notarius, C. I., and H. J. Markman. 1993. *We Can Work it Out: Making Sense of Marital Conflict.* New York: Putnam.

Ost, L. G. 1987. Applied relaxation: Description of a coping technique and review of controlled studies. *Behavior Research Therapy* 25, 397-409.

Perls, F. 1969. *Gestalt Therapy Verbatim.* Lafayette, Calif.: Real People Press.

Potter-Efron, R. 1994. *Angry All The Time.* Oakland, Calif.: New Harbinger Publications.

Smyth, L. 1996. *Treating Anxiety Disorders with a Cognitive-behavioral Exposure Based Approach and the Eye-movement Technique: The Manual.* Baltimore, Md.: Red Toad Road Company.

Sonkin, D. J., and M. Durphy. 1997. *Learning to Live Without Violence: A Handbook for Men.* Revised edition. Volcano, Calif.: Volcano Press.

Stuart, R.B. 1980. *Helping Couples Change.* New York: Guilford Press.

Wolpe, J. 1992. *The Practice of Behavior Therapy.* Needham Heights, Mass.: Allyn & Bacon.

Kim Paleg, Ph.D., is a practicing clinical psychologist specializing in couples and family therapy and codirector of the Redwood Center Psychology Associates, Inc. in Berkeley, California. She is coauthor of several relationship self-help books, including *Couple Skills* and *When Anger Hurts Your Kids*.

Matthew McKay, Ph.D., is the clinical director of Haight Ashbury Psychological Services in San Francisco. McKay is coauthor of more than 14 self-help books, including *When Anger Hurts, The Anger Control Workbook, Couple Skills,* and *The Relaxation & Stress Reduction Workbook.* In private practice, he specializes in the treatment of anger, anxiety, and depression.

Some Other
New Harbinger Titles

Thinking Pregnant, Item TKPG $13.95

Pregnancy Stories, Item PS $14.95

The Co-Parenting Survival Guide, Item CPSG $14.95

Family Guide to Emotional Wellness, Item FGEW $24.95

How to Survive and Thrive in an Empty Nest, Item NEST $13.95

Children of the Self-Absorbed, Item CSAB $14.95

The Adoption Reunion Survival Guide, Item ARSG $13.95

Undefended Love, Item UNLO $13.95

Why Can't I Be the Parent I Want to Be?, Item PRNT $12.95

Kid Cooperation, Item COOP $14.95

Breathing Room: Creating Space to Be a Couple, Item BR $14.95

Why Children Misbehave and What to do About it, Item BEHV $14.95

Couple Skills, Item SKIL $14.95

The Power of Two, Item PWR $15.95

The Queer Parent's Primer, Item QPPM $14.95

Illuminating the Heart, Item LUM $13.95

Dr. Carl Robinson's Basic Baby Care, Item DRR $10.95

The Ten Things Every Parent Needs to Know, Item KNOW $12.95

Healthy Baby, Toxic World, Item BABY $15.95

Becoming a Wise Parent for Your Grown Child, Item WISE $12.95

Stepfamily Realities, Item STEP $16.95

Why are We Still Fighting?, Item FIGH $15.95

Call **toll free, 1-800-748-6273,** or log on to our online bookstore at **www.newharbinger.com** to order. Have your Visa or Mastercard number ready. Or send a check for the titles you want to New Harbinger Publications, Inc., 5674 Shattuck Ave., Oakland, CA 94609. Include $4.50 for the first book and 75¢ for each additional book, to cover shipping and handling. (California residents please include appropriate sales tax.) Allow two to five weeks for delivery.

Prices subject to change without notice.

306.7
P156

103445

LINCOLN CHRISTIAN COLLEGE AND SEMINARY

3 4711 00168 2519